OTHER BOOKS BY JAMES W. SIRE

The Universe Next Door

How to Read Slowly

Scripture Twisting

Discipleship of the Mind

Chris Chrisman Goes to College

Why Should Anyone Believe Anything at All?

Habits of the Mind

Václav Havel

Naming the Elephant

WORLDVIEW AS A CONCEPT

A companion to
The Universe Next Door

JAMES W. SIRE

IVP Academic

An imprint of InterVarsity Press
Downers Grove, Illinois

InterVarsity Press
P.O. Box 1400, Downers Grove, IL 60515-1426
World Wide Web: www.ivpress.com
Email: email@ivpress.com

InterVarsity Press® is the book-publishing division of InterVarsity Christian Fellowship/USA®, a movement of students and faculty active on campus at hundreds of universities, colleges and schools of nursing in the United States of America, and a member movement of the International Fellowship of Evangelical Students. For information about local and regional activities, write Public Relations Dept., InterVarsity Christian Fellowship/USA, 6400 Schroeder Rd., P.O. Box 7895, Madison, WI 53707-7895, or visit the IVCF website at <www.intervarsity.org>.

Scripture quotations, unless otherwise noted, are taken from the New Revised Standard Version of the Bible, copyright 1989 by the Division of Christian Education of the National Council of the Churches of Christ in the USA. Used by permission. All rights reserved.

Cover design: Andrew Craft
Cover image: TexPhoto/iStockphoto

ISBN 978-0-8308-2779-4

Printed in the United States of America ∞

Library of Congress Cataloging-in-Publication Data

Sire, James W.
   Naming the elephant: worldview as a concept/James W. Sire.
     p. cm.
   Includes bibliographical references and index.
   ISBN 0-8308-2779-X (pbk.: alk. paper)
   1. Philosophy. I. Title
   B53.S634 2004
   140—dc22
                               2004000438

P	25	24	23	22	21	20	19	18	17	16	15	14	13	12	11	10	9
Y	25	24	23	22	21	20	19	18	17	16	15	14	13	12	11	10	

To

Donald B. Clark

(in memoriam)

and

Arthur F. Holmes

Contents

Acknowledgments

I am indebted to a host of people, many of whom I have never met but whose writings and inspiration have encouraged and upheld my interest in worldviews for almost fifty years. Of those I do know, the first among them is Donald B. Clark, then professor of English at the University of Missouri, who in a class in seventeenth-century literature introduced me to worldview thinking. Second is Arthur F. Holmes, whose comments many years ago on a simple paper encouraging students to study philosophy encouraged me to continue my own study. I was never one of his students, and he will probably not remember this first of my many encounters with him and his books, but I am pleased to acknowledge his influence as a worldview philosopher on me and many others.

David Naugle is clearly the one without whom this book would have never been begun. His masterful history of the concept of *worldview* and his own delineation of the character of the Christian worldview have provided much of the recent grist for my own mill. Thanks, David!

I am very differently indebted to Sixia Lu for confirming for me that young students can think worldviewishly and communicate their thoughts with passion and sensitivity to nuance. Her worldview paper written as an academic exercise is a tiny gem I am thankful to be able to share more widely.

Thanks too go to readers of the manuscript as it gradually developed: Richard Middleton, George Guthrie, Douglas Groothuis, Gary Deddo and, again, Arthur F. Holmes. They have not only kept me from making some rather embarrassing errors but made suggestions that required substantial further thought and research.

Finally, I want to thank Ruth Goring, who polishes my prose, and my longtime friend and editor James Hoover, who as he has improved my work has earned both my respect and my admiration.

Now with all that, I should be able to blame a lot of people for the flaws in this book. Alas, convention says I must only give credit for the good stuff and take my lumps for all the bad. And I do.

Preface

For almost fifty years I have been trying to think in worldview terms. It was worldview analysis that made the literature of the Middle Ages and the Renaissance come alive for me in graduate school at the University of Missouri. It was the history of worldviews that formed the skeleton on which as a teacher I hung the flesh of English literature. Moreover, developing a cognizance of my own worldview has provided a way of orienting not just my own thoughts but my whole take on life itself. I have, in short, long been interested in detecting the basic intellectual commitments we make as human beings, reveling in their variety, delighting in the depth of their insight when they have grasped the truth and despairing over their disastrous consequences when they have proven false.

From this context came the first edition of *The Universe Next Door* in 1976. The bulk of the book identified seven basic worldviews and then proceeded to explain what they were. I began with Christian theism as it has been largely embodied from the seventeenth century to the present. Then I tried to show how deism arose as an erosion of certain key concepts of theism. Deism, as I see it, is not so much a new worldview as what is left of theism when the personality of God is abandoned. Naturalism, then, is a further erosion of deism, retaining its optimism with regard to the autonomy of human reason. Nihilism is what is left of naturalism when it is realized that human reason, if autonomous, does not have the power to explain nearly so much as was first thought.

Existentialism—both atheistic and theistic—attempts to "go beyond nihilism," affirming the intrinsic power of the individual self to will into being its own conception of the good, the true and the beautiful or to affirm by faith what cannot be proved by reason. Eastern pantheistic monism provides for the West a fresh start that attempts to avoid the pitfalls of Western thought. New Age thought then combines Western existentialism's exaltation of the self with the Eastern notion of the deity of all things.

This is where the first edition of *The Universe Next Door* ended. The second edition, in 1988, updated the book. By 1997 it was obvious that a new twist in naturalism was taking place, and so I added a chapter on the amorphous cultural phenomenon called *postmodernism*. Postmodernism has taken a sociological and psychological twist to deny, on the one hand, the human ability to actually know reality in its essence and, on the other hand, to affirm the adequacy of human communities to construct reality by their language. One may not be able to *know* anything, but one can get along with this knowledge simply by constructing a language that works to get what one wants. Pragmatic knowledge is all one can have and all one needs.

Throughout this intellectual history I used a simple, basic definition of *worldview* which, I think, served its purpose fairly well. Somewhere in the backdrop of this definition one might detect shades of James Orr, Abraham Kuyper and Francis Schaeffer, all of whose work I had pored over in previous years. Still, in none of the three editions of *The Universe Next Door* did I explicitly reference earlier works on worldview, nor did I critically reflect on the concept of worldview itself.

After the publication of the first edition of *The Universe Next Door* in 1976, occasional comments appeared in book reviews and among my friends concerning the definition of *worldview* I had given. Then, too, several books addressing the issue of worldview appeared. Though I will make reference to others in due course, four deserve special mention. In 1983 Arthur F. Holmes's *Contours of a World View* provided the most comprehensive discussion of worldviews from a Christian standpoint. In 1984 I edited Brian Walsh and J. Richard Middleton's *The Transforming Vision: Shaping a Christian World View*; their approach differed somewhat from mine. Moreover, in 1989 the concept was analyzed in *Stained Glass: Worldviews and Social Science*, edited by Paul A. Marshall, Sander Griffoen and Richard Mouw, an important collection of essays focusing on the nature of worldviews by scholars long engaged in intellectual and cultural analysis. Finally, in 2002 David Naugle examined in detail the whole history of worldview thinking. *Worldview: The History of a Concept* summarized the literature beginning from Immanuel Kant and Wilhelm Dilthey on through James Orr and Abraham Kuyper to Francis Schaeffer and Arthur Holmes. Naugle in addition made some creative new discoveries about the nature of worldviews themselves. His book especially has been an important stimulus for the present book.

The major stimulus, however, is my own growing sense of dissatisfaction with the cursory way I have dealt with the concept of worldview. The definition in the first three editions of *The Universe Next Door* now seems inadequate to me. The present book attempts to rectify that by addressing a number of troubling questions that I have not addressed before. These questions are listed at the end of chapter one.

The time for rethinking the concept of worldview has come. If the analysis that follows is correct, four important revisions to my own earlier definition of worldview are in order. First is a recognition that a worldview is not just a set of basic concepts but a fundamental orientation of the heart. Second is an explicit insistence that at the deepest root of a worldview is its commitment to and understanding of the "really real." Third is a consideration of behavior in the determination of what one's own or another's worldview really is. Fourth is a broader understanding of how worldviews are grasped as story, not just as abstract propositions.

But this is to prejudice the case I am trying to make. Let the rethinking begin.

1

Camel, Kangaroo and Elephant

Behold the amazing elephant

Whose name is always relevant

To what we can know

And where we can go

And to all things lowly and elevant.

I do not know precisely where I got the following story, which I adapted long ago for my own purposes. In any case, I have told it often as I have tried to help students understand two central characteristics of worldviews: their *presuppositional* character and their possible answers to the most fundamental question we can ask.

CAMEL, KANGAROO AND ELEPHANT

One day a little boy came to his father. "Today the teacher showed us a big round globe. She said was a model of the world. She said the world was just surrounded by space. How can that be? Dad, what holds up the world? Why doesn't it just fall down?"

His father, knowing that this was just a child's question, gave him a child's answer: "It's a camel holds up the world, son."

The boy went away satisfied, for he trusted his father and for the moment it made sense. He'd seen pictures of camels holding up all sorts of things. So why not the world? But then he got to thinking about it and by the next day decided something was missing in his father's answer. He asked, "Dad, I was just wondering: if a camel holds up the world, what holds up the camel?"

His father now thought that he might be in trouble. So, knowing that a quick answer turneth away further questions, he said, "It's a kangaroo that holds up the camel."

Again the boy went away, but this time only for a couple of hours. Back again with his father, he asked, "Dad, if a camel holds up the world and a kangaroo holds up the camel, what holds up the kangaroo?"

This time the father realized that he was in deep trouble. So he chose the largest animal he could think of and he put a capital on it. That is, he shouted. *People believe you if you shout,* he thought. "It's an Elephant holds up the kangaroo."

"Come on, Dad!" his son retorted. "What holds up the Elephant?"

His father, in a fit of genius deriving from necessity, replied, "It's . . . it's . . . it's Elephant all the way down."

What the boy said next is not recorded. But notice two things. The father has been pushed to the logic of his first answer. If it takes something to hold up the world, then there has to be a first holder, something that doesn't require being held up—a prime foundation. If the father is to answer his son's question in the way it was asked, he is committed to naming the final foundation of reality—that is, what holds everything in existence.

Second, the father has to recognize that he has no logical way to stop the regress. He must take another tack. He must simply commit himself to the most likely one—the biggest animal he can think of, the elephant.

The story thus illustrates two characteristics of any worldview: its understanding of *prime reality* and its *pretheoretical* character. The story makes this clearer when the father takes his son's question more seriously.[1]

NATURAL OR SUPERNATURAL

In this story, the father respects his son's curiosity and intelligence. So when

---

[1] I think the origin of the story is William James, but I have yet to find it in his works. Clifford Geertz doesn't know the origin either: "There is an Indian story—at least I heard it as an Indian story—about an Englishman who, having been told that the world rested on a platform which rested on the back of an elephant which rested in turn on the back of a turtle, asked . . . what did the turtle rest on? Another turtle. And that turtle? Ah, Sahib, after that it is turtles all the way down" (Clifford Geertz, *The Interpretation of Cultures* [New York: Basic Books, 1973], pp. 28-29). This version seems to picture a worldview in which fundamental reality is an infinite regress rather than merely infinite, a flux rather than an absolute.

the son asks, "What holds the world up?" the father replies, "Gravity holds the world up, son."

"Gee, Dad, what's that?"

"The law of gravity states that the force *(F)* exerted between two bodies (such as the earth and the sun) is equal to the gravitational constant *(G)* multiplied by the product of the masses of the two bodies *(m₁, m₂)* divided by the square of the distance *(r)* between them. Here, let me write the formula for you:

$$F = Gm_1m_2/r^2$$

"Now look up *gravity* in an encyclopedia. I think you'll get the picture."

"Wow, Dad," he says after he's pored over the *World Book Encyclopedia*, "I understand the formula. It's neat. But why?"

"Well, son, the law of gravity expresses the relationship between bodies in space."

"Why, Dad?"

"Well, you see, the universe is a uniformity of natural causes, and the law of gravity expresses this uniformity in a mathematical way."

"But why is the universe uniform? What makes it be what it is? In fact, what makes it be at all?"

Now the father is at a crucial point. He has named a series of reasons, all linked logically. But he now faces a question that cannot be answered within the framework of his previous answers. In philosophic terms, his son has been asking physical questions. Now he is asking a metaphysical question: why is there something rather than nothing? In other words, what is the Animal all the way down?

The father, so it seems to me, has two basic ways to answer. He can say, "That's just the way it is." There is no further reason. There is just Being itself, brute reality, fundamental *isness*. If he takes this approach, he sides with the naturalists, who, like Carl Sagan, say, "The Cosmos is all that is or ever was or ever will be."[2]

---

[2]Carl Sagan, *Cosmos* (New York: Random House, 1980), p. 4. Theists may point out that by the principle of sufficient reason (for every effect—like the brute thereness of the universe—there must be a sufficient reason) the universe does not explain its self-sufficiency but requires a sufficient reason. This charge, however, is rejected by naturalists. The issue of sufficient reason is central to the interesting debate between Christian philosopher F. C. Copleston and ag-

But he has a second choice. He can name one more Animal, a sort of animal beyond all animals. He can say, "God made it that way." In this case, he has sided with the theists; that is, his one more Animal is a nonnatural, even supernatural, Creator.

His son can then ask again, "Why, Dad?" And his father is again at the end of his answers. Unless he has extranatural information, he must now say the same thing as the naturalist: "That's just the way it is."[3]

NAMING THE ELEPHANT

This story illustrates two primary characteristics of a worldview. First is the fact that our primary foundational commitments are just that—*commitments*, that is, presuppositions. They are what we come to when we can no longer explain why it is we are saying what we are saying. Second is the character of the question the young boy asks. He asks *what* is the case, not how we know or believe that it is the case. And the father answers in kind. I want to say from the beginning that I think the young boy asked the right question in the right way and the father likewise answered—whether as a theist or a naturalist—in the right way.

There are other ways to tell the story, other ways for the father to begin his series of answers, but his answers represent a foundational principle in the two worldviews most common in the Western and Middle Eastern world: naturalism and theism. We will examine one other story later.[4] For now my point is simple. At the base of all our thought—all our ruminations about God, ourselves and the world around us—is a worldview.

WHAT IS A WORLDVIEW?

This book arises out of two primary circumstances. The first is my own dissatisfaction with the way I defined a worldview in the first edition of *The*

---

nostic philosopher Bertrand Russell. See "A Debate on the Existence of God," in *The Existence of God*, ed. John Hick (New York: Macmillan, 1964), pp. 167-91, where Russell declares that one need find no "cause" or "explanation" for the existence of the universe: "I should say that the universe is just there, and that's all" (p. 175).

[3]Some theists, notably scholastic philosophers, would say that extranatural information is not required. If the father wanted to explain why "that's just the way it is," he could say, "God, as a perfect and necessary being, is self-explanatory. The regress ends; no further explanation is required."

[4]See chapter seven, pp. 126-27.

Universe Next Door in 1976. Because the definition is so rooted in my own mind and has been disseminated widely to students over the past quarter of a century, I will begin this book with it and then raise the issues that have seemed to me most problematic about it. In subsequent chapters I will address these issues in hopes of bringing clarity to the worldview concept and conclude with a redefinition that embodies my conclusions.

The second circumstance is the publication of David Naugle's *Worldview: The History of a Concept*, which has provided a rich source of information on the way this term and concept have developed. It has precluded my own need for extensive historical research.

What, then, is a worldview? Essentially this: A worldview is a set of presuppositions (assumptions which may be true, partially true or entirely false) which we hold (consciously or subconsciously, consistently or inconsistently) about the basic makeup of our world.

The first thing every one of us recognizes before we even begin to think at all is that something exists. In other words, all worldviews assume that something is there rather than that nothing is there. This assumption is so primary most of us don't even know we are assuming it.[5] We take it as too obvious to mention. Of course something is there!

Indeed it is. And that's just the point. If we do not recognize that, we get nowhere. Still, as with many other simple "facts" that stare us in the face, the significance may be tremendous. In this case the apprehension that something is there is the beginning of conscious life—as well as of two branches of philosophy: metaphysics (the study of being) and epistemology (the study of knowing).

What we discover quickly, however, is that once we have recognized that something is there, we have not necessarily recognized *what* that something is. And here is where worldviews begin to diverge. Some people assume (with or without thinking about it) that the only basic substance that exists is matter. For them, everything is ultimately one thing. Others agree that everything is ultimately one thing but assume that that one thing is Spirit or Soul or some such nonmaterial substance.

---

[5] Alfred North Whitehead says that some "assumptions appear so obvious that people do not know what they are assuming because no other way of putting things has ever occurred to them" (Whitehead, *Science and the Modern World* [1925; reprint, New York: Mentor, 1948], p. 49).

But we must not get lost in examples. We are now concerned with the definition of a worldview. A worldview is composed of a number of basic presuppositions, more or less consistent with each other, more or less consciously held, more or less true. These presuppositions are generally unquestioned by each of us, rarely if ever mentioned by our friends, and brought to mind only when we are challenged by a foreigner from another ideological universe.

SEVEN BASIC QUESTIONS

Another way to get at what a worldview is is to see it as our essential, rock-bottom answers to the following seven questions:

1. What is prime reality—the really real? To this we might answer God, or the gods, or the material cosmos.

2. What is the nature of external reality, that is, the world around us? Here our answers point to whether we see the world as created or autonomous, as chaotic or orderly, as matter or spirit, or whether we emphasize our subjective, personal relationship to the world or its objectivity apart from us.

3. What is a human being? To this we might answer a highly complex machine, a sleeping god, a person made in the image of God, a "naked ape."

4. What happens to persons at death? Here we might reply personal extinction, or transformation to a higher state, or reincarnation, or departure to a shadowy existence on "the other side."

5. Why is it possible to know anything at all? Sample answers include the idea that we are made in the image of an all-knowing God or that consciousness and rationality developed under the contingencies of survival in a long process of evolution.

6. How do we know what is right and wrong? Again, perhaps we are made in the image of a God whose character is good; or right and wrong are determined by human choice alone or what feels good; or the notions simply developed under an impetus toward cultural or physical survival.

7. What is the meaning of human history? To this we might answer, to realize the purposes of God or the gods, to make a paradise on earth, to prepare a people for a life in community with a loving and holy God, and so forth.

Within various basic worldviews other issues often arise. For example: Who is in charge of this world—God, or humans, or no one at all? Are we human beings determined or free? Are we alone the maker of values? Is God really good? Is God personal or impersonal? Does God exist at all? When stated in such a sequence, these questions boggle the mind. Either the answers are obvious to us and we wonder why anyone would bother to ask such questions, or else we wonder how any of them can be answered with any certainty. If we feel the answers are too obvious to consider, then we have a worldview but have no idea that many others do not share it. We should realize that we live in a pluralistic world. What is obvious to us may be "a lie from hell" to our neighbor next door. If we do not recognize that, we are certainly naive and provincial, and we have much to learn about living in today's world. Alternatively, if we feel that none of the questions can be answered without cheating or committing intellectual suicide, we have already adopted a sort of worldview—a form of skepticism that in its extreme form leads to nihilism.

The fact is that we cannot avoid assuming some answers to such questions. We will adopt either one stance or another. Refusing to adopt an explicit worldview will turn out to be itself a worldview or at least a philosophic position. In short, we are caught. So long as we live, we will live either the examined or the unexamined life.

SOME FIRST REFLECTIONS

Reflecting on this definition, one can soon see that a number of relevant issues are not addressed.

What is the history of the concept itself? Who has used it, how and why? Isn't the concept so tied to its philosophic origins in German Idealism that it imports into Christianity ideas that undermine the Christian faith? Is there any foundation in Scripture for worldview thinking? (This is addressed in chapter two.)

What is the first question a worldview should answer: What is prime reality? Or, How can anyone know anything at all? That is, which is more primary—ontology or epistemology? (This is addressed in chapter three.)

How is a worldview formed? What is the character of the foundational principles a worldview expresses? Where do they come from? Are they theoretical, pretheoretical, presuppositional or a combination of the three? (This is addressed in chapter four.)

Is a worldview primarily an intellectual system, a way of life or a story? (This is addressed in chapter five.)

What are the public and private dimensions of worldviews? What relevance does this have to their objective and subjective character? What part does behavior play in an assessment of the nature of a person's worldview? (This is addressed in chapter six.)

If the initial definition of a worldview is inadequate, what more adequate one can be given? (This is addressed in chapter seven.)

What role can worldview thinking play in assessing one's own worldview and those of others, especially in our pluralistic world? (This is addressed in chapter eight.)

2

Worldview Definitions
FROM DILTHEY TO NAUGLE

Every person carries in his head a mental model of the world—

a subjective representation of external reality.

ALVIN TOFFLER

Worldview as a concept has a rich and elaborate history.[1] The term itself is a translation from the German *Weltanschauung* and was first used by Immanuel Kant (1724-1804), but only in passing. In German Idealism and Romanticism it was used widely "to denote a set of beliefs that underlie and shape all human thought and action."[2] But it was Wilhelm Dilthey (1833-1911) who first used it as a major focus. In any case, from Kant to Ludwig Wittgenstein (1889-1951) and Francis Schaeffer (1912-1984), the concept has appeared in a variety of contexts and has adapted to or been rejected by a wide variety of worldviews, from German Idealism to Nihilism to Calvinistic Christianity.

Yet finding clear, coherent and detailed definitions of this concept in the literature is not easy. As philosopher Sander Griffeen says, "The word is used in a great many areas, ranging from the natural sciences to philosophy to theology. Authors who use it often do so without concern for proper definition, and even when definitions are given they tend to be far from precise." Some even "apologize for the vagueness of the

---

[1] Two publications are extremely helpful in delineating the details of the history of worldviews and reflecting on their nature. See David Naugle, *Worldview: The History of a Concept* (Grand Rapids, Mich.: Eerdmans, 2002), and Paul A. Marshall, Sander Griffoen and Richard Mouw, eds., *Stained Glass: Worldviews and Social Science* (Lanham, Md.: University Press of America, 1989).

[2] Peter Heslam, *Creating a Christian Worldview: Abraham Kuyper's Lectures on Calvinism* (Grand Rapids, Mich.: Eerdmans, 1998), p. 89.

term."[3] Some believe its usefulness actually resides in its vagueness.

In any case, until very recently most would have accepted this vague definition: *A worldview is the fundamental perspective from which one addresses every issue of life.* This definition leaves completely open such questions as whether a worldview is a universal, abstract philosophy or an individual, personal vision; whether finally there is one worldview or many; whether the issues addressed can be understood or not; whether a worldview is pretheoretical or theoretical; whether it is what you say you think or what you show by what you do. These issues will be taken up in later chapters.

The concept of worldview arose first in German Idealism. As such, it bears from the outset a character that Christians, if they are to use the concept, will have to either ignore or challenge. First I will summarize and review four of the salient ways worldviews have been understood by primarily secular philosophers. Then I will survey the definitions of a few key Christian worldview thinkers. From this, several important observations—perhaps conclusions—about the concept will be obvious.

SURVEY OF SECULAR WORLDVIEW DEFINITIONS

Wilhelm Dilthey. Though the term *worldview* had already been introduced in philosophic discourse by Immanuel Kant, Wilhelm Dilthey was the first to expound his own philosophy largely in terms of this concept.[4] As Michael Ermarth says, Dilthey provided "a full scale treatment of the gen-

---

[3]Sander Griffoen, "The Worldview Approach to Social Theory: Hazards and Benefits," in *Stained Glass: Worldviews and Social Science*, ed. Paul A. Marshall, Sander Griffoen and Richard Mouw (Lanham, Md.: University Press of America, 1989), p. 83. One especially obscure definition is this one by G. F. W. Hegel (1770-1831): "Starting with a specific character of this sort, there is formed and established a moral outlook on the world *[moralische Weltanschauung]* which consists in a process of relating the implicit aspect of morality and the explicit aspect. This relation presupposes both thorough reciprocal indifference and specific independence as between nature and moral purposes and activity; and also, on the other side, a conscious sense of duty as the sole essential fact, and of nature as entirely devoid of independence and essential significance of its own. The moral view of the world *[Die moralische Weltanschauung]*, the moral attitude, consists in the development of the moments which are found present in this relation of such entirely antithetic and conflicting presuppositions" (see G. F. W. Hegel, *The Phenomenology of Mind*, trans. J. B. Baillie, 2nd ed. [London: George Allen and Unwin, 1961], pp. 615-16; quoted in Naugle, *Worldview*, pp. 69-70).
[4]The word itself first appeared in Kant's *Critique of Judgment* (1790). See Naugle, *Worldview*, pp. 58-59.

esis, articulation, comparison, and development of world-views."[5] The basic role of a worldview is "to present the relationship of the human mind to the riddle of the world and life."[6] Of course there are many supposed solutions to the riddle of life, each with its own roots in individual men and women as they live and move within the flow of history. These solutions change with the person and the time.

"The ultimate root of any worldview is life itself," says Dilthey.[7] But even though each specific worldview is shaped by the character and temperament of each person, there is a common structure to their psychological life. Certain features are held by everyone—for example, "the certainty of death, the cruelty of the natural process, a general transitoriness."[8] These are the inescapable lived realities, the riddles of life, that a worldview resolves.

A worldview begins as a "cosmic picture," and then through a complex interrelation between human consciousness and the external world, a more sophisticated and detailed sense of who we are and what is the nature of that which is around us emerges. To that is added a growing sense of values. As layer upon layer of consciousness arises, eventually at the highest level one finds "a highest order of our practical behavior—a comprehensive plan of life, a highest good, the highest norms of action, an ideal of shaping one's personal life as well as that of society."[9] Naugle gives a helpful summary:

> Thus for Dilthey, the metaphysical axiological and moral structure of a worldview is derived from the constituents of the human psyche—intellect, emotion, and will respectively. Macrocosmic visions, in their composition

[5]Michael Ermarth, *William Dilthey: The Critique of Historical Reason* (Chicago: University of Chicago Press, 1978), p. 324; quoted in Naugle, *Worldview*, p. 82.
[6]Wilhelm Dilthey, *Gesammelte Schriften*, 5:406, quoted by Ramon J. Betanzos, trans., in his introduction to Wilhelm Dilthey, *Introduction to the Human Sciences: An attempt to Lay a Foundation for the Study of Society and History* (Detroit: Wayne State University Press, 1988), p. 291; quoted by Naugle, *Worldview*, p. 84.
[7]Wilhelm Dilthey, "The Types of World Views and Their Unfoldment Within the Metaphysical Systems," in *Dilthey's Philosophy of Existence: Introduction to Weltanschauungslehere*, trans. William Kluback and Martin Weinbaum (New York: Bookman Associates, 1957), p. 21. This essay contains the core of Dilthey's worldview philosophy.
[8]Naugle, *Worldview*, p. 86.
[9]Dilthey, "Types of World Views," pp. 26-27.

and content, are intrinsically reflective of the inner constitution of microcosmic human beings as they seek to illuminate the darkness of the cosmos.[ ]

Dilthey's post-Kantian metaphysics becomes clear here. What a person perceives is primarily dependent on the mind of the perceiver. We do not see what is there in the reality that confronts us; rather we understand that reality through the structures inherent in our own mind. A worldview, then, is the shaping structure of our own autonomous selves. We see what *we* see. We understand what *we* understand. Though Dilthey held that there is a common human nature and a common reality, it is nonetheless true that our worldview is *ours*, one that may be held in common with others, but only because they are like us.

As a matter of fact, of course, not everyone is like us. As Dilthey says, "World views develop under different conditions, climate, races, nationalities, determined by history and through political organization, the timebound confines of epochs and eras."[ ] So there is a multiplicity of worldviews. If this was true in Dilthey's day, so much more is it true now.

Naugle concludes, "In brief, worldviews spring from the totality of human psychological existence intellectually in the cognition of reality, affectively in the appraisal of life, and volitionally in the active performance of the will."[ ] The goal of all this is stability—a solution to the riddles of life that provides a way of successfully thinking and acting in the world.

Using this notion of worldview, then, Dilthey examines human history and finds three basic kinds of worldviews: religious, poetic and metaphysical. The metaphysical he further divides into naturalism, the idealism of freedom and objective idealism. In the end his initial trust that both reality in general and human nature in particular have significant common features seems mostly to have disappeared. Though he opts for his own form of objective idealism, Dilthey concludes, "Ultimately, nothing remains of all metaphysical systems but a condition of the soul and a world

---

[ ] Naugle, *Worldview*, p. 87. H. A. Hodges summarizes the same section this way: "Dilthey . . . analyzes a *Weltanschauung* into three structurally connected elements. The first is a belief about the nature and contents of the world of facts; the second, built on this foundation, is a system of likes and dislikes, expressed in value-judgments; and the third, resulting from the other two preceding it, is a system of desires and aversions, ends, duties, practical rules and principles" (*Wilhelm Dilthey: An Introduction* [London: Routledge & Kegan Paul, 1944], p. 92).
[ ] Dilthey, "Types of World Views," p. 27.
[ ] Naugle, *Worldview*, p. 88.

view."[15] His description and elaboration of these worldviews is rich and rewarding, but to follow it would take us too far afield of our major concern, which is to understand just what a worldview itself has been conceived to be.

In short and in my words, Dilthey conceived a worldview to be *a set of mental categories arising from deeply lived experience which essentially determines how a person understands, feels and responds in action to what he or she perceives of the surrounding world and the riddles it presents.*

Friedrich Nietzsche. Friedrich Nietzsche (1844-1900) is the boldest, if not the first, nihilist of the modern world. Reflecting on the intellectual history of his century, seeing the implications of the erosion of vibrant belief in a fully theistic concept of God—specifically the God of Abraham, Isaac, and Jacob and the Father of our Lord Jesus Christ—he infamously announced the death of God. He now saw humanity floating in an infinite sea with no fixed star by which to navigate, no port to call home, no purpose to the journey. At the same time, Nietzsche was also the boldest, if not the first, existentialist, asserting the centrality and power of the self and its attendant will. He responded to his own nihilism with his concept of the *Übermensch*, the "Superman" or "Overman," the strong individual who was to function as if he (and it was *he* that Nietzsche meant) were God—creating his own values and imposing them on others, the "last man," by the strength of his will.

With the death of God, all external standards for the true, the good and the beautiful died as well. Nietzsche was not, of course, declaring that a literal God had really died. There had never been a god of any kind. Rather, he meant that the notion of God was no longer functioning in human imagination, no longer having an effect on how people behaved. People might say they believed in God, but their thoughts and actions betrayed their functional atheism.

For Nietzsche, intellectual history is not the developing story of how people are getting closer and closer to the truth of reality. It is rather a story of changing illusions.

> What, then, is truth? A mobile army of metaphors, metonyms, and anthropomorphisms—in short, a sum of human relations, which have been enhanced, transposed, and embellished poetically and rhetorically, and which

---

[15]Dilthey, "Types of World Views," p. 74.

after long use seem firm, canonical, and obligatory to a people: truths are illusions about which one has forgotten that this is what they are; metaphors
which are worn out and without sensuous power; coins which have lost their
pictures and now matter only as metal, no longer as coins.[14]

As a result, as Naugle says, "A complete perspectivism is at the heart of
Nietzsche's philosophy."[15] Nietzsche viewed every worldview as a product
of its time, place and culture[16]:

> Nietzsche believes worldviews are cultural entities which people in a given
> geographical location and historical context are dependent upon, subordi-
> nate to, and products of. . . . A *Weltanschauung* provides this necessary,
> well-defined boundary that structures the thoughts, beliefs, and behaviors
> of a people. From the point of view of its adherents, a worldview is incon-
> testable and provides the ultimate set of standards by which things are mea-
> sured. It supplies the criteria for all thinking and engenders a basic
> understanding of the true, the good, and the beautiful. . . . Worldviews are
> nothing but reifications. They are the subjective creations of human know-
> ers in formative social contexts who ascribe their outlook to nature, God,
> law, or some other presumed authority. But they forget that they themselves
> are the creators of their own model of the world. The alleged "truth" of a
> worldview is merely an established convention—the product of linguistic
> customs and habits.[17]

Nietzsche's conception of a worldview as such is not exceptional. It is
his radical insistence that all worldviews are relative to their time and
place and circumstance that is significant. Nietzsche's historicism is no
different in some ways from that of Dilthey, but one senses in Dilthey a
longing for stability that is completely missing in Nietzsche, who, rather,
positions himself at the controls of a train that, having entered a tunnel,
will never emerge into the light. With his will as the headlight, the train

---

[14]Friedrich Nietzsche, "On Truth and Lie in an Extra-Moral Sense," in *The Portable Nietzsche*,
trans. Walter Kaufmann (New York: Viking, 1954), pp. 46-47.
[15]Naugle, *Worldview*, p. 102.
[16]Nonetheless, Nietzsche used the terms *Weltanschauung*, *Weltbild* and *Weltsicht* seventy-nine
times, says Naugle (ibid., p. 100).
[17]Ibid., p. 101; see also Peter Levine, *Nietzsche and the Crisis of the Humanities* (Albany: State
of New York University Press, 1995), esp. pp. 45-65, 187-99.

plunges ever deeper into a cavernous nothingness.[18]

Ludwig Wittgenstein. Ludwig Wittgenstein, like Hegel and Heidegger, is infamous for being cryptic and obscure. His early work bears the mark of modernity—the attempt to get one's views precisely lined up with reality. As a radical rejection of this hope, his later, postmodern work settles for "a multiplicity of mutually exclusive world pictures, forms of life, and language games." He thereby becomes "a central figure in the transition to postmodernity in which the struggle of worldviews over one and the same world is replaced by a variety of noncompetitive, linguistic constructions of reality."[19] "Whereas Plato upheld ontology and Descartes submitted epistemology as the primary concern, Wittgenstein nominated grammar and language as governing principles."[20]

In short, Wittgenstein rejected the validity of any worldview as such, for each and every one of them pretends to what is impossible—an intellectual grasp of reality as it really is. What we have instead is "an approach to the world that consists of unverifiable models of life, language, culture and meaning."[21]

We meet here a problem in terminology. In one important sense—a sense I want to maintain—everyone, including Wittgenstein, has a worldview. Any rejection of that notion is self-refuting. It's like saying, "There are no absolutes; everything is relative," a statement that, if true, is false, in other words, self-referentially incoherent. Wittgenstein clearly makes statements about reality, even if the reality the statements describe is solely linguistic or the statements are only to be judged by their usefulness for getting what one wants. That is, his statements about the nature of language are not just truth claims to be placed noncombatively against opposite truth claims, as if one claim were as true as the other. Rather, they are statements about the actual nature of language. If they are not, they assert nothing and do not need to be taken seriously by anyone.

Put another way, Wittgenstein rejects the notion that anyone can have knowledge about any nonlinguistic reality. In other words, Wittgenstein

---

[18]This image comes from Friedrich Dürrenmatt, "The Tunnel," in *A Casebook on Existentialism*, ed. William V. Spauos (New York: Thomas Y. Crowell, 1966), pp. 54-64.
[19]Naugle, *Worldview*, pp. 152-53.
[20]Ibid., p. 149.
[21]Ibid., p. 157.

takes no "view" of either ontology ("what is") or epistemology ("how one can know"); he has only a hermeneutic ("how one can understand and use language").

Perhaps we can state Wittgenstein's worldview (though he would not call it a worldview) like this: *A worldview is a way of thinking about reality that rejects the notion that one can have "knowledge" of objective reality (that is, know any "truth" about any nonlinguistic reality) and thus limits knowable reality to the language one finds useful in getting what one wants.*

Instead of worldview *(Weltanschauung)* Wittgenstein prefers to speak of "world picture" *(Weltbild)*. Nonetheless, *world picture* as he uses the term seems synonymous with *worldview.*

> [World picture facts] are doubt-proof and serve . . . as the "axis," "river-bed," "scaffolding," and "hinges" of a particular way of thinking and acting. These reified world pictures, creating reality as they do, thus form for their adherents a kind of pseudometaphysics in which they live, and move, and have their being. . . . World pictures in Wittgensteinian terms . . . are not to be conceived as epistemically credible constructs competing for rational adherence, but as webs of belief which must be set forth in effective terms to be received as a way of organizing reality. In the final analysis, all one can say about one's outlook on the world is that this is what we are, this is what we understand, and this is what we do.[22]

However we are to understand Wittgenstein's complicated views, it is clear that he has rejected their ability to give us a clear foundation for knowledge of the surrounding world. Constructed of language, they in turn construct reality for us. We see what they allow us to see.

Michel Foucault. Michel Foucault (1926-1984) uses the terms *episteme* and *worldview*, sometimes in contrast, sometimes almost as synonyms. The distinction is probably important in understanding the nuances of his philosophy, but I will treat his remarks about one to include his views of the other. He writes, "Episteme may be suspected of being something like a world-view, a slice of history common to all branches of knowledge, which imposes on each one the same norms and postulates, a general stage of rea-

---

[22]Ibid., p. 161.

son, a certain structure of thought that all men of a particular period cannot escape—a great body of legislation written once and for all by some autonomous hand."[23] An episteme involves "an inescapable set of rules and regulations, a way of reasoning, a pattern of thinking, a body of laws that generate and govern all patterns of knowing."[24]

What makes his understanding of worldviews worth our attention here is the connection he makes between them and power:

> He sets before his readers a view of the world in which human beings are trapped within language structures and knowledge regimes with no possibility of escape. Every human discourse is a power play, every social arrangement oppressive, and every cultural setting tyrannical.[25]

Foucault has no time for truth about objective reality. There are only discourses, and each of them is a play for power.

> "Truth" is to be understood as a system of ordered procedures for the production, regulation, distribution, circulation, and operation of statements.
>
> "Truth" is linked in a circular relation with systems of power which produce and sustain it, and to effects of power which it induces and which extends it. A "regime" of truth.[26]

"In skeptical Foucaultian terms, worldviews are merely the linguistic constructions of a power elite. They are the facades of an absentee reality, and function as effective means of social oppression."[27] Or, in other words, "worldviews are nothing but pseudointerpretations of an ultimate reality all dressed up in a linguistic power suit."[28]

SURVEY OF CHRISTIAN WORLDVIEW DEFINITIONS

With these definitions in the background, let us turn to a few Christian

---

[23]Michel Foucault, *The Archaeology of Knowledge*, trans. A. M. Sheridan Smith (New York: Random House/Pantheon, 1972), p. 15; quoted in Naugle, *Worldview*, p. 181.

[24]Naugle, *Worldview*, pp. 181-82.

[25]Ibid., p. 183.

[26]Michel Foucault, "Truth and Power," in *The Foucault Reader*, ed. Paul Rabinow (New York: Pantheon, 1984), p. 74.

[27]Naugle, *Worldview*, p. 184.

[28]Ibid.

thinkers who found the worldview concept especially valuable: James Orr, Abraham Kuyper, Herman Dooyeweerd, James Olthuis, Al Wolters, Ronald Nash and John Kok. The insights of Brian J. Walsh and Richard J. Middleton will be considered later (chapter five).

James Orr. James Orr (1844-1913), a Scottish Presbyterian theologian, first introduced worldview thinking into Christian theology in his 1890-1891 Kerr Lectures at the United Presbyterian College in Edinburgh, published as *The Christian View of God and the World.* Orr was well aware of the German source of the concept and adapted it for his own apologetic purposes.[29] His main goal was to provide a complete, coherent, rationally defensible exposition of Christianity, one that would stand up to the intellectual and cultural challenges of his day. The concept of worldview provided precisely the tool of analysis and exposition that fit the task. "It is the Christian view of things in general which is attacked, and it is by an exposition and vindication of the Christian view of things as a whole that the attack can be met."[30]

Orr then set out to justify Christian belief by showing how the Christian faith addresses all the major issues of concern to human flourishing. "That the Christian faith may be conceived as a christocentric, self-authenticating system of biblical truth characterized by inner integrity, rational coherence, empirical verisimilitude, and existential power is one of his most distinctive contributions."[31]

His notion of *worldview* itself was taken from the general understanding of *Weltanschauung* or *Weltansicht* prevailing at the time. To wit: A worldview is "the widest view which the mind can take of things in an effort to grasp them together as a whole from the standpoint of some particular philosophy or theology."[32] Orr calls on Edward Caird for an elaboration: "Beneath and beyond all the detail in our ideas of things, there is a certain *esprit d'ensemble*, a general conception of the world without and the world within, in which these details [of experience] gather to a head."[33] Not only do these details come to a head, they do so coherently: "Everywhere the minds of

[29]James Orr, *The Christian View of God and the World* (Grand Rapids, Mich.: Eerdmans, 1954), pp. 4-5, 365-70.
[30]Ibid., p. 4.
[31]Naugle, *Worldview,* p. 13.
[32]Orr, *Christian View,* p. 3.
[33]Edward Caird, *Social Philosophy of Comte,* p. 24, quoted in Orr, *Christian View,* p. 6. Caird (1835-1908) was a Scottish philosopher holding an idealist notion of reality.

men are opening to the conception that, whatever else the universe is, it is one—one set of laws holds the whole together—one order reigns through all. Everywhere, accordingly, we see a straining after a universal point of view—a grouping and grasping of things together in their unity."[34]

Worldviews have their source "deep in the constitution of human nature" and involve both the intellect and the actions we perform. Orr then goes on to discuss at some length the peculiar characteristics of the Christian worldview, doing so in largely theological terms, such as "God," "human beings," "sin," "redemption" and "human destiny," but focusing throughout and in particular on the incarnation of God in Christ.

Orr's views have been seminal, helping shape the way the notion of a Christian worldview has developed.

Abraham Kuyper. Another, perhaps even more important figure standing at the beginning of Christian worldview thinking is Abraham Kuyper. Kuyper (1837-1920) was a contemporary of James Orr and familiar with his work. In his 1889 Stone Foundation Lectures at Princeton University, published as *Lectures on Calvinism*, Kuyper extended Orr's approach, presenting Calvinist Christianity as a comprehensive worldview, or in Kuyper's terminology an all-embracing "life system." Every worldview, Kuyper holds, must address "three fundamental relations of all human existence: viz., our relation to *God*, to *man* and to the *world*."[35] Kuyper goes on to detail these:

> For our relation *to God:* an immediate fellowship of man with the Eternal, independently of priest or church. For the relation of man *to man:* the recognition in each person of human worth, which is by virtue of his creation after the Divine likeness, and therefore of the equality of all men before God and his magistrate. And for our relation *to the world:* the recognition that in the whole world the curse is restrained by grace, that the life of the world is to be honored in its independence, and that we must, in every domain, discover the treasures and develop the potencies hidden by God in nature and in human life.[36]

Unlike Orr, however, Kuyper does not follow this with a theology built on this threefold set of relationships. Instead, in the next four lectures he

---

[34]Orr, *Christian View*, p. 8.
[35]Abraham Kuyper, *Lectures on Calvinism* (Grand Rapids, Mich.: Eerdmans, 1931), p. 31.
[36]Ibid.

explains how the Christian worldview relates to, illuminates and stimulates culture to its highest peak of perfection in religion, politics, science and art. He concludes with a ringing call to face the future with a Calvinist worldview firmly embedded in our thoughts and life.

> Philosophy, psychology, aesthetics, jurisprudence, the social sciences literature, and even the medical and natural sciences, each and all of these, when philosophically conceived, go back to principles and of necessity even the question must be put with much more penetrating seriousness than hitherto, whether the ontological and anthropological principles that reign supreme in the present method of these sciences are in agreement with the principles of Calvinism, or are at variance with their very essence.[37]

One element of Kuyper's worldview concept is especially important: his notion that every worldview has a single conception from which the whole worldview flows. Kuyper scholar Peter S. Heslam writes that, even before Kuyper gave the Stone Foundation Lectures, Kuyper held that there is a "need for all thought to proceed from a single principle, a 'fixed point of departure.'"[38] The relevance of this to the present study will become apparent later.

Herman Dooyeweerd. Herman Dooyeweerd (1894-1977) is perhaps the most philosophic of all Christian worldview thinkers. At the same time, he is the most insistent that theoretical thought does not lie at the basis of one's worldview. More fundamental than any worldview that can be delineated by ideas and propositions is the religious or faith orientation of the heart. "For Dooyeweerd, all human endeavor stems not from worldview, but from the spiritual commitments of the heart."[39]

---

[37]Ibid., p. 194.

[38]Heslam, *Creating a Christian Worldview*, p. 92. Heslam points out that Orr too "had an independent, unified, and coherent worldview derived from a central belief or principle" (p. 93).

[39]Naugle, *Worldview*, p. 26. Yet Dooyeweerd's conception of the heart is quite vague, much more so than Naugle's, since, as Ronald Nash says, "He [Dooyeweerd] tells us that the heart should not be identified with any of the following: (1) man's emotions or feelings; (2) man's intellect or reason; (3) the temporal function of faith (even though it is true that man believes with his heart); (4) or with any immaterial substance (or material substance, for that matter)" (*Dooyeweerd and the Amsterdam Philosophy* [Grand Rapids, Mich.: Zondervan, 1962], p. 91). Arthur Holmes, as well, has associated Dooyeweerd's notion of worldview with the biblical concept of heart as the "unifying core" of a human being (*Contours of a World View* [Grand Rapids, Mich.: Eerdmans, 1983], p. 32).

There are only two basic commitments, leading to two basic conditions of life: "man converted to God" and "man averted from God." The commitment one makes is "decisive for all life and thought."[40] From the former comes the Christian worldview not so much as a matter of theoretical thought expressed in propositions but as a deeply rooted commitment of the heart: "Theory and practice are a product of the will, not the intellect; of the heart, not the head."[41]

Dooyeweerd identifies two religious ground motives that "give contents to the central mainspring of the entire attitude of life and thought."[42]

> [The first is] the dynamis of the Holy Ghost. [This] brings man into the relationship of sonship to the Divine Father. Its religious ground motive is that of the Divine Word-Revelation, which is the key to the understanding of the Holy Scripture: the motive of *creation, fall, and redemption by Jesus Christ in the communion of the Holy Ghost.*
>
> The second central mainspring is that of the spirit of apostasy from the true God.[43]

As Dooyeweerd understands them, worldviews are not philosophic systems; rather they are *pretheoretical* commitments and are in direct contact not so much with the mind as with the "heart," with experience, with life as lived. Still, in the final analysis, as Naugle points out, the close connection Dooyeweerd makes between "the ground motive of the Holy Spirit" and the biblical themes of creation, fall and redemption makes it hard to see how this ground motive is distinguished from a Christian worldview. I will return to this notion in chapter seven (pp. 127-28).

RECENT EVANGELICAL DEFINITIONS

For several decades after Kuyper, the worldview concept was not much discussed by Christian theologians and philosophers. The Reformed

---

[40]Jacob Klapwijk, "On Worldviews and Philosophy," in *Stained Glass: Worldviews and Social Science*, ed. Paul A. Marshall, Sander Griffoen and Richard Mouw (Lanham, Md.: University Press of America, 1989), p. 51.

[41]Naugle, *Worldview*, p. 27.

[42]Herman Dooyeweerd, *A New Critique of Theoretical Thought*, trans. David H. Freeman and William S. Young (no city: Presbyterian & Reformed, 1969), 1:61.

[43]Ibid.

community centered in Calvin College, however, kept the notion alive, and in the 1960s it began to emerge as well in the work of philosophers associated with the Christian Studies Institute in Toronto, under the direct influence of Herman Dooyeweerd and the memory of Abraham Kuyper.

Today there is a general consensus among evangelicals who write about worldviews that Orr, Kuyper and, occasionally, Dooyeweerd have influenced their own understanding. Common to the first two and their modern counterparts are the notions that worldviews are beliefs that are (1) rooted in pretheoretical and presuppositional concepts that are the foundation for all one's thought and action, (2) comprehensive in scope, (3) ideally though not necessarily logically coherent, (4) related in some positive way to reality, that is, to the way all things and relations really are, (5) though not necessarily irrational, nonetheless fundamentally a matter of commitment that is not finally provable by reason.[44]

James Olthuis. Perhaps the fullest and clearest brief definition of *worldview* is that of Canadian philosopher James Olthuis:

> A worldview (or vision of life) is a framework or set of fundamental beliefs through which we view the world and our calling and future in it. This vision need not be fully articulated: it may be so internalized that it goes largely unquestioned; it may not be explicitly developed into a systematic conception of life; it may not be theoretically deepened into a philosophy; it may not even be codified into creedal form; it may be greatly refined through cultural-historical development. Nevertheless, this vision is a channel for the ultimate beliefs which give direction and meaning to life. It is the integrative and interpretative framework by which order and disorder are judged; it is the stan-

---

[44]A host of Christian thinkers from across the academic disciplines use *worldview* in this general way. A few examples will suffice: Steven Garber, *The Fabric of Faithfulness: Weaving Together Belief and Behavior During the University Years* (Downers Grove, Ill.: InterVarsity Press, 1996), esp. pp. 108-24; Armand M. Nicholi Jr., *The Question of God* (New York: Free Press, 2002), p. 7; Douglas Groothuis, *Unmasking the New Age* (Downers Grove, Ill.: InterVarsity Press, 1986), p. 17; W. Gary Phillips and William E. Brown, *Making Sense of Your World* (Chicago: Moody Press, 1991), pp. 42-43; Clifford Williams, *The Life of the Mind: A Christian Perspective* (Grand Rapids, Mich.: Baker Academic, 2002), p. 18; faculty contributors to *Shaping a Christian Worldview: The Foundations of Christian Higher Education*, ed. David S. Dockery and Gregory Alan Thornbury (Nashville: Broadman & Holman, 2002), pp. 1-15, 249-54, 280-97.

dard by which reality is managed and pursued; it is the set of hinges on which all our everyday thinking and doing turns.[45]

Olthuis goes on to comment on how a worldview relates to both persons and their communities:

Although a vision of life is held only by individuals, it is communal in scope and structure. Since a worldview gives the terms of reference by which the world and our place in it can be structured and illumined, a worldview binds its adherents together into community. Allegiance to a common vision promotes the integration of individuals into a group. At times communality of vision not only binds people together, but also, ironically, provides them with the tools and vocabulary to advance with greater sophistication their internal differences.[46]

Albert M. Wolters. Canadian theologian Albert M. Wolters similarly defines *worldview* but does so more simply:

For our purposes *worldview* will be defined as "the comprehensive framework of one's basic beliefs about things." . . . A worldview is a matter of the shared everyday experience of humankind, an inescapable component of all human knowing, and as such it is nonscientific, or rather (since scientific knowing is always dependent on the intuitive knowing of our everyday experience) *prescientific* in nature. It belongs to an order of cognition more basic than that of science or theory. Just as aesthetics presupposes some innate sense of the beautiful and legal theory presupposes a fundamental notion of justice, so theology and philosophy presuppose a pretheoretical perspective on the world. They give a scientific elaboration of a worldview.[47]

Ronald Nash. One of the clearest expositions of the worldview concept is that of Ronald Nash. He says, "In its simplest terms, a worldview is a set of beliefs about the most important issues in life. . . . [It] is a conceptual scheme by which we consciously or unconsciously place or fit everything

---

[45]James H. Olthuis, "On Worldviews," in *Stained Glass: Worldviews and Social Science*, ed. Paul A. Marshall, Sander Griffoen and Richard Mouw (Lanham, Md.: University Press of America, 1989), p. 29.
[46]Ibid.
[47]Albert M. Wolters, *Creation Regained: Biblical Basics for a Reformational Worldview* (Grand Rapids, Mich.: Eerdmans, 1985), pp. 2, 9.

we believe and by which we interpret and judge reality."[48] This theoretical scheme is founded on nontheoretical notions, though these notions can be identified and thought about and changes can be consciously made. Nash identifies five key elements of a comprehensive worldview: one's understanding of God, of ultimate reality (by which he means the world in its essence), knowledge, ethics and humankind.[49]

John H. Kok. Philosopher John H. Kok's definition deserves mention because it shores up, more than most others I have seen, the gap between the purely intellectual and the embodied character of worldviews.

> A worldview may well be defined as one's comprehensive framework of basic beliefs about things, but our *talk* (confessed beliefs or cognitive claims) is one thing, and our *walk* (operative beliefs) is another and even more important thing. A lived worldview defines one's basic convictions; it defines what one is ready to live and die for.[50]

A worldview, he says, is "more than a collection of concepts." It is as well "the vision that one gets from home or from the public square, the vision that one has assimilated for oneself with difficulty or grown up with, so much so that one almost takes it for granted. It is not a scientific or theoretic conception but a view, a sense—of God, the world, life, human nature, one's neighbor, oneself—that has become second nature."[51]

WORLDVIEW AS A MATTER OF WORLDVIEW

Before beginning the present study of worldviews, I had the distinct sensation that how one conceived of a worldview depended on one's worldview. This brief survey confirms that suspicion.

The secular story. What we see in the sequence from Kant and Dilthey to Foucault is the shift from modernity to postmodernity. The concept of a worldview itself arises at the height of modernity as represented by Kant, who extended the autonomy of human reason to its peak. For him the very nature of any reality that can be known is tied inextricably to the nature of

[48]Ronald Nash, *Worldviews in Conflict* (Grand Rapids, Mich.: Zondervan, 1992), p. 16.
[49]Ibid., pp. 26-30.
[50]John H. Kok, "Learning to Teach from Within a Christian Perspective," *Pro Rege*, June 2003,
    p. 12. Kok is professor of philosophy and dean of humanities at Dordt College.
[51]Ibid., p. 14.

the human mind. Total reality consists of the noumenal (a transcendent realm) and the phenomenal (an immanent realm). The noumenal is inaccessible to the human mind. But the phenomenal can be known, because the human mind contains the categories by which the phenomenal can be structured and thus understood.

It is this basic conception that stands behind Dilthey's understanding of worldview. For Dilthey, in my words, a worldview is *a set of mental categories arising from deeply lived experience which essentially determine how a person understands, feels and responds in action to what he or she perceives of the surrounding world and the riddles it presents.*

What we know is determined by the pretheoretical categories we use to know. So while a worldview may result in a set of ideas or beliefs about fundamental reality, the worldview itself is composed of the categories by which we see.

Kant was a *modern* philosopher. Like Descartes he assumed a universality in human nature. The categories were understood to be universal constants. The riddles of life are the same for all: death, cruelty, transitoriness. One's worldview results from the struggle to understand these and other existential conundrums. One's view of the world, then, is shaped by encounter with life. In his early work Dilthey, like Kant, seems to have believed that this provided the basis for an understanding of reality that was universal.

Later Dilthey recognized that this is not the case. As Naugle says, worldviews "are developed under radically different conditions by radically different kinds of people."[32] So they become as numerous as the number of people in the world. Dilthey thus became a historicist; he came to see human knowledge as inextricably bound to time, place and culture.[33] With this insight we are at the doorway to postmodernity.

With Nietzsche we are there. For Nietzsche, worldviews—all claims to knowledge and understanding—are perspectival. Truth itself is a "mobile army of metaphors." Nothing can be stated that does not depend on a point of view that is no more likely to be related to reality than any other point of view.

---

[32]Naugle, *Worldview,* p. 87.

[33]Dilthey seems not to have noticed the self-referential incoherence of this position: If all worldviews are a product of their time and place, so is his, and so are the specific views that flesh it out, including his view that all worldviews are a product of time and place. This is the situation of much postmodern thought. See James W. Sire, *The Universe Next Door,* 4th ed. (Downers Grove, Ill.: InterVarsity Press, 2004), chap. 9.

In his early work, Wittgenstein was as modern as Descartes. But in his later work he steps into the postmodern world: The solid, objective world of people and things becomes linguistic. We invent ways of using language (language games), he says, that allow us to move about in a world we do not directly know. Our language allows us to act with some success in getting what we want.

It is not that there *is* nothing but language. There are many things that are not language, and they are important. It is just that claims to knowledge cannot be confirmed by checking those claims against reality. They can be evaluated only by how well they work. We may seem to know, but what we seem to know has been constructed for us by the language we use.

Foucault takes us to the final consequences of postmodernity. He adds the notion that all language is a claim to power. Any worldview as a statement about reality is neither true nor false in any objective sense. Its truth lies solely in its ability to secure power for oneself or the community of people who affirm it.

The irony is that any notion that a worldview forms a foundation for what we really know undermines itself. Even Foucault's implicit claim to know how language functions is undermined. If all language is solely a power play, then so is the language by which Foucault explains language. Therefore, unless one wants to play the language game on the side of Foucault and by so doing secure whatever power one can, there is no particular reason to agree with Foucault.

In any case, if this were the only story in the history of the concept of worldview, the history would end in the death of the concept—or at least the death of any significance to the concept. Nihilism, however, does not stop intellectuals from writing, only from making sense.

The Christian story. The history of the worldview concept has another story—one deriving from its employment by Christian thinkers from the end of the nineteenth century on into the twenty-first. This story begins with James Orr.

By his own admission Orr borrowed the bulk of his concept from German Idealists such as Wilhelm Dilthey and the Scottish Idealist Edward Caird. Caird, whom he quotes, speaks of a "general *conception* of the world" (which sounds idealist). Orr says a worldview is "the widest view which the mind can take of things" (which sounds idealist), but adds, "in an effort to grasp them together as a whole" (which sounds realist), and further, "from the standpoint of some particular philosophy or theology" (which again sounds idealist).

But Orr's focus is on the world that is to be grasped, not the nature of the grasp itself (and that is realist). There is "one set of laws," and "one order reigns through all." There is a "grouping and grasping of things together in their unity" (again realist). Moreover, as Orr develops the particularly Christian worldview, he is not interested in the categories by which the world is grasped but in the character of the world itself. When Orr turns to the elaboration of the Christian worldview in nine brief sections, each of them begins with "The Christian view affirms . . ."[54] For example:

> I. First, the Christian view affirms the existence of a Personal, Ethical, Self-Revealing God.[55]

This sentence makes an ontological claim. So does the following:

> II. The Christian view affirms the creation of the world by God. His immanent presence in it, His transcendence over it, and His holy and wise government of it for moral ends.[56]

The same thing is true of Abraham Kuyper. His "life system" concerned "three fundamental relations" considered as such, relations that were taken to exist in reality, not just in our "picture" of reality. Quite striking is Kuyper's notion of a *sensus divinitatis* that is present in each of us and allows a direct access to God. God, then, "enters *into immediate fellowship with the creature*."[57] Neither theoretical thought nor language intervenes. "At every moment of our existence, our entire spiritual life rests in God himself."[58] One can't get more realistic, more ontological, than that.

This realist emphasis re-emerges in Olthuis, Wolters and Nash. In fact, the focus of most, if not all, of the evangelical Christian definitions of *worldview* is never on the *categories* by which we grasp God, humanity and the

---

[54]Orr, *Christian View*, pp. 32-34.
[55]Ibid., p. 32.
[56]Ibid.
[57]Kuyper, *Lectures on Calvinism*, pp. 21, 46.
[58]Ibid., p. 21.

world but on what God, humanity and the world actually, objectively (i.e., outside our thought life) are. So in one sense the story of Christian worldview thinking from Orr to the present has no plot. The concept of a worldview is largely frozen in time. Or would be if it were not for David Naugle. Because he adds a unique flavor, we will look more deeply at his work.

A new synthesis: David Naugle. With Naugle the Christian story of worldview enters a new phase. On the one hand, like other Christian worldview thinkers, Naugle grounds his definition of the Christian worldview in ontology. On the other hand, he acknowledges the shift in perspective from ontology to hermeneutics, adding to his definition the notion that a worldview is characterized by a "semiotic system of narrative signs."[59]

First, observe the ontological foundation. Other worldview analysts such as Olthuis and Holmes are conscious of the close links between their notion of worldview and that of the nineteenth-century Idealist philosophers, but they have done little to address the potential danger of this link. Naugle has taken the threat seriously—especially the subjective character of worldviews and the resulting relativism.

It is one thing for Dilthey to begin with the Enlightenment trust in the unity of truth and the autonomy of human reason, and then to find the former undermined by the latter. The question of "whose reason" or "whose rationality" inevitably arises when different reasoners address the same issue and come to contradictory conclusions. Reason itself, so it comes to be seen, is tied to time and place and person. For one who does not believe in a God who reveals truth to his creation, relativism may be an unwanted result of the autonomy of human reason, but it does not conflict with anything but human desire. For a Christian, relativism challenges the very heart of Christian commitment. It is not just that Christians, like everyone (as Aristotle would say), desire to know the truth. It is not that they must believe they have a full grasp of the truth; they know that sin has a negative noetic effect. But Christians do believe that part of the truth about truth is that truth is one. Two contradictory statements can't both be true. There is an exclusivity to truth.

This notion is implicit in the Hebrew Scriptures, but it becomes startlingly

---

[59]Naugle, *Worldview*, p. 253.

explicit in the teaching of Jesus. Take the notion of what happens after death.

When he knew that he did not have long to live, Jesus told his disciples, "Do not let your hearts be troubled. Believe in God, believe also in me" (Jn 14:1). Then he told them that there is a life after death for them, that he is going away to make a place for them with his Father, that he is doing this so that eventually they can be with him.

When Thomas, one of his disciples, was confused, Jesus said, "I am the way, and the truth, and the life. No one comes to the Father except through me" (Jn 14:6).

This is neither the language nor the concept of relativism. It is a direct claim to truth that cannot rationally be countered or balanced by its opposite. What Jesus said is either true or false. It may not be easy to assemble evidence for its truth or falsity, but that does not change the nature of the claim itself.

If the concept of worldview commits one to relativism, it cannot be used as a tool within the workshop of a Christian mind. Naugle knows this and counters it directly in the first proposition of his definition of *worldview* from a Christian standpoint:

> "Worldview" in a Christian perspective implies the objective existence of the trinitarian God whose essential character establishes the moral order of the universe and whose word, wisdom and law define and govern all aspects of created existence.[60]

For Naugle the first fundamental presupposition of the Christian faith is ontological—a statement about what is, about the really real. Naugle is not alone in placing ontology first in order. That has been the case for Christian worldview thinkers from Orr to the present. Naugle presents his position clearly:

> God . . . is that ultimate reality whose trinitarian nature, personal character, moral excellence, wonderful works and sovereign rule constitute the objective reference point for all reality. . . . The meaning of the universe and the authority to determine it are not open questions since both are fixed in the existence and character of God. Relativism and subjectivism are thereby excluded.[61]

---

[60] Ibid., p. 260; italics his.
[61] Ibid., pp. 261-62.

There is, therefore, what Naugle calls a *creational objectivity* to the Christian tradition, "an absolutist perspective on life that is real, true, and good."[62]

Second, harking back to the German Idealists, Naugle acknowledges the subjective nature of worldviews:

> "Worldview" in a Christian perspective implies that human beings as God's image and likeness are anchored and integrated in the heart as the subjective sphere of consciousness which is decisive for shaping a vision of life and fulfilling the function typically ascribed to the notion of Weltanschauung.[63]

Naugle, so far as I have been able to determine, is the first worldview analyst to emphasize the striking similarity between the biblical concept of the heart and the worldview concept. It is an insight worth lauding, for this refutes the charge that the German Idealist source of the worldview concept necessarily imports Idealism into Christian thought. Rather it illustrates a motif long recognized in Christian history, the spoiling of the Egyptians—that is, accessing the true insights of the pagan world for the development of Christian theology. Truth is truth wherever it is found.[64]

---

[62]Ibid., p. 266.

[63]Ibid., p. 267; italics his.

[64]Naugle's insight that what German Idealism calls a Weltanschauung is almost identical with what the Bible terms "heart" goes a long way toward answering Gregory A. Clark's charge that "the notion of worldviewness first becomes possible with the work of Kant" ("The Nature of Conversion: How the Rhetoric of Worldview Philosophy Can Betray Evangelicals," in *The Nature of Confession: Evangelicals and Liberals in Conversation*, ed. Timothy R. Phillips and Dennis Okholm [Downers Grove, Ill.: InterVarsity Press, 1996], p. 205). Clark holds that the notion of Weltanschauung is so utterly idealistic that biblical thought cannot be seen in worldview terms. Mark Noll, on the other hand, says, "The construction of Christian world views has been an ongoing task throughout the history of the church" ("Christian World Views and Some Lessons of History," in *The Making of a Christian Mind: A Christian World View and the Academic Enterprise*, ed. Arthur Holmes [Downers Grove, Ill.: InterVarsity Press, 1985], p. 30). The apostle Paul was aware of worldviews that contrasted with his own in his speech in Athens (Acts 17:16-34). Even the creation account in Genesis may have been cast in terms that deliberately countered the Babylonian concept of creation (Joseph Spradley, "A Christian View of the Physical World," in *Making of a Christian Mind*, p. 58). In any case, the truth or aptness of a concept is not dependent on how old it is or where it came from, but on whether it comports with reality. Moreover, I find no reason to think that most Christian definitions of *worldview*, including my own original definition or the revised version proposed in the present book, are essentially idealistic.

The ancient Hebrews before Christ and the Christians afterward saw the heart as the core of the human personality. In the Hebrew Scriptures the word itself *(leb, lebab)* occurs 855 times. It is used to denote not only the physical organ but "the central, defining element of the human person. In short it is seen as the seat of the intellectual, . . . affective, . . . volitional, . . . and religious life of a human being."[65]

A few examples cited by Naugle are in order:

Intellectual
For the LORD gives wisdom . . .
Wisdom will come into your heart,
    and knowledge will be pleasant to your soul. (Prov 2:6, 10)

Affective
[God tells Moses that Moses's brother is on the way to meet him], "and when he sees you his heart will be glad." (Ex 4:14)

Volitional
[David prayed], O LORD, the God of Abraham, Isaac, and Israel, our ancestors, keep forever such purposes and thoughts in the hearts of your people, and direct their hearts toward you. (1 Chron 29:18)

In the New Testament "the heart is the psychic center of human affections, . . . the source of the spiritual life, . . . and the seat of the intellect and the will."[66]

Psychic center of human affections
[Jesus says to his disciples], Do not let your hearts be troubled. (Jn 14:1)

Source of the spiritual life
[Peter says to Simon the sorcerer], You have no part or share in this, for your heart is not right before God. (Acts 8:21)

Seat of the intellect
For though they knew God, they did not honor him as God or give thanks to him, but they became futile in their thinking, and their senseless minds [*kardia*] were darkened. (Rom 1:21)

---

[65]Naugle, *Worldview*, p. 268.
[66]Ibid.

Naugle continues, "Jesus shares this point of view, teaching that the heart is the spiritual nucleus of the person about which life orbits."[67]

> [Jesus says not to store up treasure.] For where your treasure is, there your heart will be also. (Mt 6:21)

In short, "the heart and its content as the center of human consciousness creates and constitutes what we commonly refer to as a *Weltanschauung*."[68] How then does the heart become constituted? How is it shaped and formed? Naugle puts it this way:

> Into the heart go the issues of life. Before the springs of life flow *out of* the heart, something must first and even continue to flow *into it*. . . . Things are internal-
> ized *before* they are externalized. . . . Certainly from childhood on a torrential amount of content is poured into the reservoir of the heart from seemingly un-
> limited sources of varying quality, some of it pure, some of it polluted.[69]

Naugle then lists such "heart-shaping influences" as "religious, philosophical, and cultural traditions; socioeconomic conditions; various institutions such as marriage, the family, and education; human relations and friendships; vocational choice and work experience; psychological and physical health; sexual experiences; warfare; and so on." There is indeed an *interactive or reciprocal* relationship with the external world.

In such a way a worldview is formed and continually shaped and modified by one's life in the world—in crisis and in ordinary times.

Likewise, "out of the heart go the issues of life."[70]

> Once the heart of an individual is formed by the powerful forces of both na-
> ture and nurture, it constitutes the presuppositional basis of life. Presupposi-
> tions are those first principles that most people take for granted. They are multifaceted in character, and, knit together, they make up the most basic psychic layer of life. They constitute the background logic for all thinking and doing.[71]

---

[67] Ibid., p. 269.
[68] Ibid., p. 270.
[69] Ibid., p. 271.
[70] Ibid.
[71] Ibid., p. 272.

On the one hand, our actions act to form and re-form our heart. On the other hand, our actions display what the content of our heart actually has come to be. Who we are is not just who we think or proclaim ourselves to be. It is who we show ourselves to be by the way we behave. Likewise, what our worldview actually is is not just what we think it is but what we show it is. As the letter of James proclaims, "What good is it, my brothers and sisters, if you say you have faith but do not have works? . . . Show me your faith without works, and I by my works will show you my faith" (Jas 2:14, 18).

When Jesus' disciples were eating food without ceremonially washing their hands, the Pharisees objected. The disciples were being unfaithful to the law, they said. But Jesus replied by giving a number of illustrations of how the Pharisees were able to keep the letter of the law and yet violate its spirit. Then he said,

> There is nothing outside a person that by going in can defile, but the things that come out are what defile. . . . It is what comes out of a person that defiles. For it is from within, from the human heart, that evil intentions come: fornication, theft, murder, adultery, avarice, wickedness, deceit, licentiousness, envy, slander, pride, folly. All these evil things come from within, and they defile a person. (Mk 7:15, 20-23)

It is clear from the context that Jesus is affirming the close connection between the heart—the central core of a human being, characterized by a fully operative worldview—and the actions one takes. The issue is an issue of the heart. Worldviews have both an objective referent and a deeply subjective character.

Thus far, it seems to me, Naugle has brilliantly brought together the insights of Idealism and biblical Christianity. He further strengthens the biblical features of a Christian worldview by specifically noting the "catastrophic effects of sin on the human heart and mind," the "cosmic spiritual warfare in which the truth about reality and the meaning of life is at stake," "the gracious inbreaking of the kingdom of God into human history in the person and work of Jesus Christ," which makes a "knowledge of the true God" and his creation possible to believers. These particular concepts are, however, unique to the Christian worldview and need not concern us as characteristics of all worldviews.

But Naugle makes a third move that concerns all worldviews, not just those purporting to be Christian. Notice what he adds to his definition of a worldview as such:

> A worldview is a semiotic system of narrative signs that has a significant in-
> fluence on the fundamental human activities of reasoning, interpreting,
> and knowing.[2]

Elsewhere he says that a worldview is "a *semiotic phenomenon*," "a system of signs generating a symbolic world," "a network of *narrative* signs," "a semiotic system of world-interpreting stories . . . [that] provides a foundation or governing platform upon which people think, interpret, and know."[3]

In semiotic terms his fullest definition is this:

> A worldview, then, is a semiotic system of narrative signs that creates the de-
> finitive symbolic universe which is responsible in the main for the shape of
> a variety of life-determining, human practices. It creates the channels in
> which the waters of reason flow. It establishes the horizon of an interpreter's
> point of view by which texts of all types are understood. It is that mental me-
> dium by which the world is known. The human heart is its home, and it
> provides a home for the human heart. At the end of the day it is hard to con-
> ceive of a more important human or cultural reality, theoretically or prac-
> tically, than the semiotic system of narrative signs that makes up a
> worldview.[4]

At first Naugle appears to be defining a worldview primarily as language. A worldview is a *semiotic system of narrative signs*, he says. If this were taken without being set within his earlier characterization of a worldview as both realistically objective and mentally subjective, a worldview would not be a *set of mental categories* (Dilthey), a *way of thinking* (Wittgenstein), the *widest view a mind can take* (Orr), a *set of fundamental beliefs* (Olthuis, Wolters, Nash), a *comprehensive framework of one's basic beliefs* (Wolters) or my own *set of presuppositions*. None of these focus on the linguistic char-acter of these categories or frameworks or beliefs—that is, the fact that a worldview can be expressed in a language.

---

[2]Ibid., p. 253.
[3]Ibid., p. 291.
[4]Ibid., p. 330.

Naugle presents a detailed biblical and philosophic argument for his semiotic definition, basing his conclusions on suggestions from a wide range of philosophers, theologians, psychologists and even a folklorist. Among them are Augustine, Umberto Eco, Hans-Georg Gadamer, C. S. Peirce, Ernst Cassirer, Rollo May, Bruno Bettelheim and Linda Dégh. Key to his view is the idea that God has imbued the whole of the cosmos with meaning and human beings with the ability to grasp that meaning. "The entire universe should be conceived pansemiotically and interpreted as the sign of God and his glory and power. . . . The totality of creation is divine iconography. Everything in this enchanted sacramental symbol-friendly universe is drenched with *sacred* signs."[75] As the psalmist says, "The heavens are telling the glory of God" (Ps 19:1). Human beings themselves, says Peirce, "are thoroughly semiotic in their basic nature," and Naugle appears to agree.

In short, Naugle combines the notion of the Christian worldview as (1) an objective *ontological* commitment to the triune, personal and transcendent God of Scripture, (2) a subjective, deeply embedded, heart-oriented perspective and (3) a semiotic system of narrative signs. I take this to be his attempt to preserve the commonsense notion that reality is objective in essence, subjective in apprehension, and able to be meaningfully comprehended and communicated in language.

The main point to be made here, however, is that while Naugle may appear to place semiotics (or meaning or language) prior to what we ordinarily take to be ontology, he does not do so. I am assured by Naugle himself that he does not want the semiotic character of a worldview to displace his commitment to the notion that ontology is prior to both epistemology and hermeneutics.[76] He cites the following preface to his presentation of a worldview as a semiotic system:

> Thus, against the background of the previous chapter with its affirmations of an objective reality rooted in God, the central significance of the human heart, the dynamics of sin and spiritual warfare, and the hope of Christian grace and redemption, we undertake these philosophical reflections in an at-

---

[75]Ibid., p. 293.
[76]David Naugle, personal communication.

tempt to deepen our understanding of the nature of a worldview and its influence on all things."

In short, Naugle has added a perspective to worldview analysis that deserves wide attention. It will be seen later in this book to be very like my own.

A Base from Which to Move Forward

This brief history of worldviews as understood by both Christians and others provides a good foundation for further rumination about the character of worldviews. We will begin that rumination by considering the issue of "first things." What is the most foundational issue of all? Is it being or knowing or, perhaps, meaning? To this issue we now turn.

"Naugle, *Worldview*, p. 292. He adds this in his personal communication: "Ontologically grounded worldviews, regardless of whether that ontology is theistic, deistic, naturalistic, pantheistic, and so on, consist of a system of signs, especially narrative ones, that reside in the human heart and there generate a perspective on reality. That of which wvs are made is a system of signs; that about which they speak is being or reality. Formally, they are semiotic, materially they are established ontologically."

3

First Things First

BEING OR KNOWING

God said to Moses, "I AM WHO I AM."

He said further,

"Thus you shall to say to the Israelites:

'I AM has sent me to you.'"

EXODUS 3:14

When the young boy asked his father, "What holds the world up?" the question demanded an ontological answer. The boy was not asking about the authority on which his father would base his answer (epistemology). Nor was he asking about the meaning or intentionality—if any—of the world (its purpose for being there). He was not wondering whether there was any value to the world (ethics). He was instead asking a question about *what* the nature of the universe is. What makes this globe relate to the rest of the cosmos such that it can seem to hang in space?

Whether the father gives the naturalist answer (matter and energy in complex but orderly unity) or the theist answer (God made it that way), the answer is ontological. Throughout the history of Western thought till the seventeenth century, the ontological question has been implicitly understood to be primary. That something exists has been taken as a starting point. The first question then becomes, What is it that is there? Self-reflection replies, "I am there, and something other than me seems to be there too. Who or what am I? And is there any other? If so, what?" These are all ontological questions.

Other questions soon follow: How is it that I am able to know what is there? Why is it there? Why am I here? Am I responsible for what I do? What should I do? What makes being here worth the effort to continue to be here?

In my first formulation in *The Universe Next Door*, there are seven prime questions. I have listed them in chapter one; I list them again here for easy reference:

1. What is prime reality—the really real?

2. What is the nature of external reality, that is, the world around us?

3. What is a human being?

4. What happens to persons at death?

5. Why is it possible to know anything at all?

6. How do we know what is right and wrong?

7. What is the meaning of human history?

Let us assume for the moment that these seven questions come close to exhausting the issues addressed by a worldview. There is another question that quickly arises: Does the sequence of questions make a difference? The quick answer is yes—a profound difference. A substantial answer is the main purpose of this chapter.

Perhaps the best way to demonstrate the importance of putting first things first is to see what happens under two different circumstances: (1) when ontology precedes epistemology and (2) when epistemology precedes ontology.

Ontology First

Both traditional Jewish theism and traditional Christian theism have always seen the Infinite-Personal God as most basic form of what is. God, at the most fundamental level, is what it means to *be*. That is, they have put ontology before epistemology.

When Moses turned aside to see a burning bush that was not consumed by the flame, a voice identified itself as the traditional, tribal God of the Hebrew people, the God of Moses' fathers—"the God of Abraham, the God of Isaac, and the God of Jacob" (Ex 3:6). When Moses asked for God's name, God replied, "I AM WHO I AM. This is what you are to say to the Israelites: 'I AM has sent me to you'" (Ex 3:14 NIV). *I AM*: one can get no more fundamentally real than that. I AM is not to be equated with anything within the created order. He is not the god of war or the moon goddess or the spirit of the Nile, one among many. He is single and sole. He is what it is *to be*.[1]

Of course the God of the Hebrew and Christian Scriptures does not remain without character. He is far more than bare being. Even in the Scripture in which God identifies himself as That Which Is—i.e., that which by its very nature could never not be—God shows himself as the tribal God of Moses' family, the God of Abraham, Isaac and Jacob. This God is no vague ethical principle or mere infinite force. He is fully personal. He calls Abraham out of Ur of the Chaldees. He accepts the worship of Abraham. He engages himself in the whole history of the Hebrew people, speaking personally to and through his prophets.

It is not necessary here to show the way by which the biblical concept of God unfolds in the history of the Jews and Christians. But a few high points emphasizing the ontological aspects of biblical revelation will confirm its centrality to the Christian worldview.

The first chapter of Genesis declares that God was "in the beginning," that unlike the gods of the surrounding nations, he is not a part of the cosmos. He is rather the Creator of the universe (the heavens and the earth) and of human beings, declared to be so like him that they are "in his image."

Moses is told that if he obeys God by returning to Egypt to bring the Israelites out of captivity, God will meet him on a mountain in the wilderness. Moses obeys, and through the course of his obedience he learns to trust God. In fact he becomes so engaged with God that he wants to see him face to face. "Show me your glory," he asks (Ex 33:18). God warns him that no one can see him fully and live, but he puts Moses in a crack of a huge rock and then passes by so that Moses can see his back. In the process he declares to Moses who he is. This declaration is rich in intellectual content but contains an enigma that will not be explained till Jesus unlocks its secret:

> The LORD, the LORD,
> a God merciful and gracious,
> slow to anger,
> and abounding in steadfast love and faithfulness,

---

[1]Scholastic philosophers would say that in him and him alone essence and existence are one (see E. L. Mascall, *He Who Is: A Study in Traditional Theism* [London: Libra, 1966], p. 13).

keeping steadfast love for the thousandth generation,
forgiving iniquity and transgression and sin,
yet by no means clearing the guilty,
but visiting the iniquity of the parents
upon the children
and the children's children,
to the third and the fourth generation. (Ex 34:6-7)

The enigma—God as love and God as judge—is untangled only when Jesus, very God of very God, takes on himself the sins of the world. As Paul says, "For our sake he made him to be sin who knew no sin, so that in him we might become the righteousness of God" (2 Cor 5:21).

The point here is that the biblical concept of God is rich in content. One of the clearest formulations of this concept is given in the Westminster Confession:

> There is but one only living and true God, who is infinite in being and per-
> fection, a most pure spirit, invisible, without body, parts, or passions, immu-
> table, immense, eternal, incomprehensible, almighty, most wise, most holy,
> most free, most absolute, working all things according to the counsel of his
> own immutable and most righteous will, for his own glory; most loving, gra-
> cious, merciful, long-suffering, abundant in goodness and truth, forgiving in-
> iquity, transgressions, and sin; the rewarder of them that diligently seek him;
> and withal most just and terrible in his judgments; hating all sin, and who
> will by no means clear the guilty. (2.1)

The second and third sections (2.2-3) of the Confession then further un-pack the notion, commenting on the all-sufficient character of the Trinity in terms of goodness, power and knowledge.

Not everyone who can be said to have a Christian worldview will express (or even be able to express) their concept in such detailed and abstract lan-guage. In a much briefer way, the following definition gets, I think, to the essence:

> God is the infinite, personal (triune), transcendent and immanent, omni-
> scient, sovereign and good being who created the universe.[2]

---

[2]This definition is based on the first two propositions of Christian theism in James W. Sire, *The Universe Next Door*, 3rd ed. (Downers Grove, Ill.: InterVarsity Press, 1997), pp. 23, 26.

EPISTEMOLOGY SECOND

With this concept as the foundation of the Christian worldview, it is easy to see that the answers to the subsequent six worldview questions will be limited. If prime reality is the biblical God, for example, then it is neither what anyone imagines it to be nor what scientists say it is; the cosmos is what it has been made to be. Its nature and character are determined by God. Moreover, people—each individual and all of them together—are who God has made them to be, not who they think they are or declare themselves to be. John Henry Newman put this point well: even though God as Creator is infinitely separate from his creation, "yet He has so implicated Himself with it and taken it into His very bosom by His presence in it, His providence over it, His impressions upon it, and His influences through it, that we cannot truly or fully contemplate it without contemplating Him."[3]

All of the universe bears a distinct relationship to God. "Religious Truth is not a portion, but a condition of general knowledge," Newman says.[4] Moreover, the universe is knowable.

Epistemology is predicated on the nature of what is, not on an autonomous ability, human reason disengaged from God. Moreover, there is no dichotomy between religious knowledge and secular knowledge. As Newman says, "All knowledge forms one whole, because its subject matter is one; for the universe in its length and breadth is so intimately knit together that we cannot separate off portion from portion, and operation from operation, except by mental abstraction."[5]

If prime reality is the biblical God, ethics will not be based on humanity's highest aspirations but will be grounded in the character of God as ultimate goodness. Human purpose will not be self-determined by any person, community, nation or multinational group but will be predetermined by God.

In the biblical worldview, in short, everything is first and foremost determined by the nature and character of God. It cannot be said too

---

[3]John Henry Newman, *The Idea of a University*, ed. Frank M. Turner (New Haven, Conn.: Yale University Press, 1996), p. 37.
[4]Ibid., p. 57.
[5]Ibid., p. 45.

strongly: *Ontology precedes epistemology*. Though it may not appear to be so at first, to turn this around and presuppose the epistemology determines ontology is devastating to the Christian worldview.

When the Scriptures turn to epistemology, they do so with the assumption of the existence of God. The primary text here is the opening of the Gospel of John:

> In the beginning was the Word, and the Word was with God, and the Word was God. He was in the beginning with God. All things came into being through him, and without him not one thing came into being. What has come into being in him was life, and the life was the light of all people. The light shines in the darkness, and the darkness did not overcome it. (Jn 1:1-5)

God as existent in the beginning or "from everlasting" (Ps 93:2) underlies both the existence of the universe and its determinate nature. It is the Word, Logos (the very principle of rationality, purpose and meaning), that characterizes God himself. And it is by the Word that all things were made. In other words, all things have a particularly determinate character. They are one thing and not another; there is order, not chaos.

As Josef Pieper says:

> Everything that has *being* is by its very nature—which means, by reason of its being *real*—also knowable. . . . All existing things originated in the creative and inventive mind of God and *consequently*, when they were conceived and then also "spoken," they received in themselves, as their essence, the quality of a "spoken word," the character, therefore, to be in principle understandable and intelligible.[6]

George MacDonald, the novelist-theologian whom C. S. Lewis thought to be "closer, or more continually close, to the Spirit of Christ Himself" than any other writer, expands on the same notion:

> I believe that every fact in nature is a revelation of God, is there such as it is because God is such as He is; and I suspect that all its facts impress us so that we learn God unconsciously. From the moment when first we come

---

[6]Josef Pieper, *In Defense of Philosophy*, trans. Lothar Krauth (San Francisco: Ignatius, 1992), pp. 74-75.

into contact with the world, it is to us a revelation of God, His things seen, by which we come to know the things unseen.[ ]

Human knowledge is possible because he who created and knows all things exhaustively is also the "light of all people" (Jn 1:4). Christ is "the true light, which enlightens everyone" (Jn 1:9). That is why we can know. Ontology—the existence of an omniscient God who creates us in his image—is the foundation for epistemology.

Ontological priority even governs the evangel. All four Gospels are bent on answering one primary question: Who is Jesus? It is not what he did or even what he said that is the first matter of importance. It is who he was. If he is understood to be who he was, then his teaching will be powerful and existential, not just abstractly true, and his life, death and resurrection will be among the most significant events of the cosmos.

Finally we should note the rich connection between theology and science. For what we study in every academic field is made by God and sustained by his presence. "He sustains all things by his powerful word" (Heb 1:3).

The character of this world is what it has been made to be. As John says, the Logos made the world, that is, reasonability/intelligibility/meaningfulness is characteristic of the world. There is reason to believe that despite its human-mind-boggling complexity, there is intelligible order and structure behind it all.

So what is the nature of fundamental reality? What is Being? It is God in his awesome personal array of omniscience, omnipotence, omnipresence and goodness. We can understand the universe because an understanding God made it to be understood.

EPISTEMOLOGY FIRST

Of course, in his revelation of himself to human beings, God sometimes gives reasons this revelation is to be trusted. These reasons are often linked to actions that his prophets are to perform. Moses, for example, was told to

[ ]George MacDonald, *Creation in Christ*, ed. Rolland Hein (Wheaton, Ill.: Harold Shaw, 1976), p. 145; Lewis's comment on MacDonald comes from his preface to *George MacDonald: An Anthology* and is quoted on the cover of *Creation in Christ*.

lead the Israelites out of Egypt and into the desert. If he did so, God would be with him and give supernatural signs of God's approval and his power to free the Israelites from bondage. Some of those signs were given to Moses before he stepped out on this seemingly impossible task (Exodus 3 and following chapters); others came after he had begun to obey. Jesus, too, gave the religious leaders reasons for his claim to be the One sent from God (Jn 5:31-47). And the Gospel of John records seven signs that further justify belief in Jesus as God incarnate. The Bible assumes the existence of God; it does not try to prove it.

But all of these presuppose the God who reveals. What happens when establishing the foundation for knowledge precedes confidence in Being itself? What happens when epistemology preempts ontology? The story can be told historically. We will begin with Descartes.[5]

The seventeenth century was plagued with skepticism. Religious diversity was beginning to run rampant: Luther's tribe was increasing across Europe, rivaled by Calvin's tribe, and both were answered by the Counter Reformation. The basic intellectual unity of the Christian worldview was being shattered from within with contending parties willing to do battle for their version of truth. It is no wonder that thoughtful people wondered if there was any way to get to a truth that could be held with final certainty. Enter Descartes.

René Descartes (1596-1650), a fully orthodox Catholic philosopher, made a stellar attempt to find a way to knowledge that could not possibly be

---

[5]Gregory A. Clark says, "The idea of 'worldviewness' emerges to solve a set of problems in epistemology. . . . The idea of a 'worldview' has its natural home in the field of post-Kantian philosophy" ("The Nature of Conversion: How the Rhetoric of Worldview Philosophy Can Betray Evangelicals," in *The Nature of Confession: Evangelicals and Liberals in Conversation*, ed. Timothy R. Phillips and Dennis Okholm [Downers Grove, Ill.: InterVarsity Press, 1996], p. 203). This may well be a fact of intellectual history, but it does not mean that any specific worldview must itself make the epistemological issue the first of its concerns. A Christian worldview does not need to do this in order to be a worldview, and in my estimation it should not do so. Neither do I think that a Christian conception of a worldview should put the epistemological issue first. A Christian is *first* of all one who affirms the existence of an infinite-personal God, not one who takes the Bible as a revelation of God. A naturalist is first of all one who holds that matter (or matter plus energy in a complex relationship) is all there is, not one who holds to the autonomy of human reason or any other such epistemological notion. The precise concept of worldview is worldview dependent. No worldview excepting an idealist worldview is necessarily wedded to idealism, post-Kantian or otherwise.

false. His concept of God was identical to that of Aquinas.[9] What he was searching for was a way to show that this concept was certainly true. So he devised a method of radical doubt in order to find the certain truth.[10]

In brief, the argument is this: God might not exist; the external world might not exist; but at least I must exist because I think. To wit: *I think; therefore I am*. After all, even if the content of what I think is not itself so, I am something because I am aware. Even if I doubt that I am, I must be or I wouldn't be doubting.

On this rests the case Descartes made for the certainty that at least he — a thinking thing — exists. He went on to analyze what made this conclusion valid, concluding that its clearness and distinctness and the impossibility to conclude otherwise guaranteed its truth. The certitude of this knowledge rests not on any revelation either directly from God or indirectly from a book, but solely on human reason (the consciousness of thinking) itself. One can know this on one's own. Hence the autonomy of human reason.

That there are a variety of ways to understand Descartes's argument is evident from the vast literature that has grown up around it.[11] I will cut to the chase. First, if *I think; therefore I am* is taken as an argument, it is circular and therefore invalid. The conclusion ("I") is already in the premise. But there is good reason to think that Descartes did not mean the statement to

---

[9]Forty years ago as a graduate student I was able to convince my philosophy professor in a term paper that this is the case. Had I read Étienne Gilson's *God and Philosophy* (New Haven, Conn.: Yale University Press, 1941), I might have added this quote: "True enough, the God in whom, as a Christian, Descartes believed was the selfsame God whom, as a philosopher, he knew to be the supreme cause of all things; the fact however remains that, as a philosopher, Descartes had no use for God taken in himself and in his absolute self-sufficient perfection. To him God was an object of religious faith; what was an object of knowledge was God taken as the highest among the 'Principles of Philosophy'" (pp. 36-37).

[10]René Descartes, "Meditation I," in *The Philosophical Works of Descartes*, trans. Elizabeth S. Haldane and G. R. T. Ross (n.p.: Dover, 1955), 1:145. Elsewhere Descartes writes, "We should busy ourselves with no object about which we cannot attain a certitude equal to that of the demonstrations of Arithmetic and Geometry" ("Rules," in *Philosophical Works of Descartes*, 1:5). As Frederick Copleston puts Descartes's view, "There is only one kind of knowledge, certain and evident knowledge." See Frederick Copleston, *A History of Philosophy*, vol. 4, *Descartes to Leibnitz* (London: Burns, Oates & Washbourne, 1958), p. 70.

[11]See, for example, Bernard Williams, *Descartes: The Project of Pure Enquiry* (Harmondsworth, U.K.: Penguin, 1978); Margaret Dauler Wilson, *Descartes* (London: Routledge, 1978); and Stephen Gaukroger, *Descartes: An Intellectual Biography* (New York: Oxford University Press, 1995).

be an argument, but rather the description of an intuition.[12]

If it is an intuition, what is it that is intuited? Descartes would seem to say the "I" or ego, the seat of consciousness. Put another way, *Consciousness is; therefore a conscious one (I) exists.* This does not, of course, mean that everything the I is conscious of exists. I may have a consciousness of the other—the world in general—but the world may not exist. I may have a rich imaginative life including not just a seeming experience of the world around but mathematical systems, philosophic ideas, memories of music and so forth. But none of them may be outside my mind. Descartes realizes this, and so he constructs an argument to demonstrate that under certain circumstances what one is conscious of necessarily exists.

He reflects on what makes him so certain that thinking is going on. He concludes that it is the *clearness* and *distinctness* of the idea. It is so clear and distinct, so unable to be thought otherwise, that there must be a reality to sustain it. Of course, Descartes has other clear and distinct ideas, the most significant of which is an idea of God: "By the name God I understand a substance that is infinite [eternal, immutable], independent, all-knowing, all-powerful, and by which I myself and everything else, if anything else does exist, have been created."[13]

This notion, Descartes argues, could not have been solely a product of his own fallible mind; the finite cannot from itself form a concept of the infinite. Rather it has to have a concept of the infinite in order to grasp the finite, and that must have derived from the infinite. Therefore the idea of God as an infinite being must have been given him by God. In short, God as such a being must exist.

In a second line of argument, Descartes considers whether he who has the idea of God can exist if God does not exist. He concludes that he himself would have to have the perfections of God (such as infinity) to have been able to cause himself to have the idea of God. He obviously does not possess those perfections. Since he does have ideas of those perfections, God must have caused them. Therefore God exists.[14]

---

[12]Williams, *Descartes*, p. 89.

[13]René Descartes, "Meditation III," in *The Philosophical Works of Descartes*, trans. Elizabeth S. Haldane and G. R. T. Ross (n.p.: Dover, 1955), 1:165.

[14]The arguments I have merely outlined are examined in detail by Williams, *Descartes*, pp. 130-62, and Copleston, *History of Philosophy*, 4:92-115.

I exist and God exists, concludes Descartes, but what about the material world? Since such a God exists, he would not deceive. And since I have a clear and distinct sense that there is such a world (even though I may make errors about just what that material world is), the existence of that world is certain. The very strong conviction that there is an objective world proves that an external world exists.

What I have summarized, very briefly to be sure, is the argument in Descartes's first four meditations. From the autonomy of the self (the thinker) comes the certitude first of one's own existence. Based on that, God's existence is certain. And based on that, the existence of the external world is certain. Epistemology precedes ontology.

In "Meditation V," Descartes returns to the issue of God's existence, this time giving his own version of the ontological argument—an argument asserting the inherent necessity for there to be a single being whose essence is existence, from whom derive all other beings in the universe. This argument leads him to conclude that unless such a being exists, his own reasoning has no reason to be considered certain:

> And so I very clearly recognise that the certainty and truth of all knowledge depends alone on the knowledge of the true God, in so much that, before I knew Him, I could not have a perfect knowledge of any other thing. And now that I know Him I have the means of acquiring a perfect knowledge of an infinitude of things, not only of those which relate to God Himself and other intellectual matters, but also of those which pertain to corporeal nature in so far as it is the object of pure mathematics.[15]

Descartes has moved a very long way from his radical doubt that anything at all exists, including himself. He has moved, one could say, from existential angst to intellectual arrogance.[16] Here in tone as well as substance is the core of the modern mind: the declaration that human reason (while known and experienced to be fallible), resting on the existence of God, whose existence

---

[15]Descartes, "Meditation V," 1:184.

[16]This may be more rhetorical than accurate. It is difficult to believe that Descartes suffered what twentieth-century existentialists would call angst. Still, it was no mere game; Descartes based his whole philosophy on the *cogito*. If he is wrong here, his entire philosophical enterprise is in question. Descartes himself says, "The destruction of the foundations of necessity brings with it the downfall of the rest of the edifice" (Descartes, "Meditation I," 1:145).

is proved by that human reason, has the ability to acquire "perfect knowledge of an infinitude of things." The Enlightenment confidence in the capacity and power of the human mind does not stem directly from the specifics of Descartes's argument, but it certainly was a major impetus to that end.

Hosts of subsequent philosophers have poked holes both in Descartes's three arguments for the existence of God and in his argument for the certitude of his own existence. The weaker of the arguments are clearly those for the existence of God.

First, the first two arguments for the existence of God assume the notion of sufficient reason (causality)—that for any given thing, idea or event there must be a reason sufficient to bring it about. While there are both common sense and sophisticated reasons that lend credibility to the principle, Descartes does not subject it to his method of radical doubt. Of course the notion of sufficient reason can be doubted; perhaps the world is chaotic or indeterminate (e.g, one reading of the Heisenberg uncertainty principle). The principle of sufficient reason does not have to be untrue in order for the conclusion of the argument to be less than certain; it only needs to be able to be doubted, and like the existence of the external world, it can be. Descartes's radical doubt is not so radical as he seems to believe.

Second, these two arguments require that the idea of God be clear and distinct. Is that the case with the notion of God as "a substance that is infinite [eternal, immutable], independent, all-knowing, all-powerful, and by which I myself and everything else, if anything else does exist, have been created"? If it is not clear and distinct (and it may not be), that disqualifies it as a part of the argument. Besides, what is a *clear* and *distinct* idea? The notion has, so far as I know, never been clarified sufficiently. That is, the notion itself does not seem to be clear and distinct. My idea of a pink elephant or a unicorn actually seems more clear and distinct than my idea of such a complex being as is necessary for the argument. But unicorns and pink elephants—so far as I know—do not exist.

Third, Descartes's ontological argument in "Meditation V" seems to come out of the blue. It does not depend on any of the arguments in the first four meditations. And what he draws from it is that only if God exists can he trust his own reasoning. That would have to include the foundational arguments he gives for the certitude of his own existence.

John Cottingham is correct: "The importance of God in the Cartesian system can scarcely be overstressed."[17] While he began from certain self-knowledge, Descartes realized that he could not sustain his philosophy solely on the self-certainty of his own existence—that is, the autonomy of his human reason. God needed to exist in order for Descartes to trust his own reasoning. At the same time, making the certainty of God's existence rest on the certainty of his own existence was the first step toward the undermining of trust in human reason. For if the initial argument or intuition is in error, or if it yields too weak a plank on which to erect a case for God's existence, then the certitude of God's existence is undermined and skepticism results. At this point, one also has no case for the certainty of the existence of the natural world.[18]

It appears then that Descartes has not made his case for the existence of God. And with that goes his case for the certitude of human knowledge. But the problem goes deeper than that. The very notion that *I think; therefore I am* makes a case for the existence of an ego certain enough to sustain an epistemology that justifies certain knowledge is itself suspect. Let us see why.

COGITO, ERGO SUM

On the surface, *I think; therefore I am* seems to be a valid argument. Centuries before, Augustine used it in both his dialogue on free will and his handbook on Christian doctrine.

> AUGUSTINE: First tell me whether you are absolutely certain that you are alive.
>
> EVODIUS: What could be more certain than that?
>
> AUGUSTINE: Then you can distinguish between being alive and knowing that you are alive?

---

[17]John Cottingham, "Descartes, René," in *The Cambridge Dictionary of Philosophy*, ed. Robert Audi (Cambridge: Cambridge University Press, 1995), p. 195.

[18]Leszek Kolakowski, critiquing Edmund Husserl's attempt to solve the problem posed by the inadequacy of Descartes's *cogito* argument, puts it this way: "Husserl's monodology is for me another example of the logical hopelessness of all philosophical endeavors which start from subjectivity and try to restore the path toward the common world" (*Husserl and the Search for Certitude* [Chicago: University of Chicago Press, 1987], p. 79).

EVODIUS: I know that nothing knows that it is alive unless it is in fact alive.[19]

That, then, settles the matter for Augustine. He does not examine just what it is that constitutes the "I" that knows it is alive. Nor does he do so in his handbook of Christian doctrine:

> It is impossible that any one should be ignorant that he is alive, seeing that if he be not alive it is impossible for him to be ignorant; for not knowledge merely, but ignorance too, can be an attribute only of the living. But, forsooth, they think that by not acknowledging that they are alive they avoid error, when even their very error proves that they are alive, since one who is not alive cannot err. As, then, it is not only true, but certain, that we are alive, so there are many other things both true and certain; and God forbid that it should ever be called wisdom, and not the height of folly, to refuse assent to these.[20]

The first part of Augustine's argument seems fair enough. Surely if I ask the question, "Do I exist?" then I exist. But I do not yet know who or what I am. What characterizes the asker? All that can be established by the argument taken strictly is that an asker has asked a question about his or her own existence, the answer to which must be yes. This asker could be dreaming, in which case anything else that the asker might wish to know would be suspect. The asker could be the only conscious being in existence. The asker's reasoning could on all other issues be utterly disconnected from reality.

Descartes needs to establish the ability of the "I" (ego, self) to reason from certain self-awareness to the existence of that which is other than himself—the world and God. Through self-reflection Descartes observes that his self-awareness is characterized by being *clear* and *distinct*. It is this, he says, that gives him the intellectual certainty that he seeks. But surely, even if we know what it is to have a clear and distinct idea (something I am unwilling to grant), there is no particular reason to think that is what guarantees the existence of that which is so clear and distinct. Descartes might reply that God would not deceive us by allowing us to have a clear and distinct idea that did not comport with reality, but that would be to assume

---

[19]Augustine, *On Free Choice of the Will*, trans. Thomas Williams (Indianapolis: Hackett, 1993), p. 12 (1.7).
[20]Augustine, *The Enchiridion on Faith, Hope and Love*, ed. Henry Paolucci (Washington, D.C.: Regnery Gateway, 1961), pp. 26-27 (20).

what Descartes is trying to prove—the existence of a God who would not deceive. The argument would be circular. John Cottingham puts it this way:

> If the reliability of the clear and distinct perceptions of the intellect depends on our knowledge of God, then how can that knowledge be established in the first place? If the answer is that we can prove God's existence from premises that we clearly and distinctly perceive, then this seems circular; for how are we entitled, at this stage, to assume that our clear and distinct perceptions are reliable?[21]

There would seem to be no way for Descartes to escape from the lonely confines of an ego with no boundaries and therefore no definition.

Nietzsche sees this and much more in his devastating critique of Descartes's *cogito:*

> For, formerly, one believed in "the soul" as one believed in grammar, and the grammatical subject: one said, "I" is the condition, "think" is the predicate and conditioned—thinking is an activity to which thought *must* supply a subject as cause. Then one tried with admirable perseverance and cunning to get out of this net—and asked whether the opposite might not be the case: "think" the condition, "I" the conditioned; "I" in that case [am] only a synthesis which is *made* by thinking.[22]

Nietzsche often shocks the intellect. He does so here. Is the "I" the active agent, the one who thinks? Or is the "I" simply produced by thought? Is it only thinking that exists?[23]

If it seems too extreme, too odd, to think that there could be "thinking" without a "thinker," then notice how it is we perceive that thinking is going on. Whether or not the mind can think without language, the moment that we detect thinking, language is involved. We know we think because we

[21]Cottingham, "Descartes," p. 195.
[22]Friedrich Nietzsche, *Beyond Good and Evil,* in *The Basic Writings of Nietzsche,* ed. Walter Kaufmann (New York: Modern Library, 1969), sec. 54, p. 257.
[23]Kolakowski echoes Nietzsche's critique: "Descartes's blunder consists in his decision that he could doubt the existence of the world but not his own existence—that his Ego was given him in absolute immediacy and he was thus a thinking substance. But in pure phenomena no thinking substance appears. Therefore we have to eliminate the substantial Ego as well.... This phenomena *is* given, but not so the fact that it is 'mine'" (*Husserl and the Search,* p. 38).

can put our thoughts into words. The words we put them into come with all the baggage of a specific language—a specific grammar and vocabulary. Perhaps when I say, "I think," I am saying this in a language (English) that requires a predicate *(think)* to have a subject *(I* or *she* or *they)*. When I use Latin the word *cogito* contains with its inflection both the predicate and the subject. In either case, if I say only the word *think*, I have not said anything. *Think* alone does not imply any subject. But it is just such a subject that I am trying to prove exists. Perhaps "I" is only a creation of language; perhaps the self is only a linguistic construct.

Nietzsche's blows have struck home. Descartes's doubt has not been sufficiently radical. The "I" of the *cogito* may just be the *cogito*, the thinking thing (if it need be a thing) constructed by the thinking.[24]

More important for us at the beginning of the twenty-first century is the view expressed by some postmodernists. Consider first Richard Rorty's proclamation that language (a necessary condition of conscious thought) just happens:

> The orchids, when their time came, were no less marvelous for the sheer contingency of this necessary condition of their existence. Analogously, for all we know, or should care, Aristotle's metaphorical use of *ousia,* Saint Paul's metaphorical use of *agape* and Newton's metaphorical use of *gravitas* were the results of some cosmic rays scrambling the fine structure of some crucial neurons in their respective brains. Or, more plausibly, they were the result of some odd episodes in infancy—by idiosyncratic trauma. It hardly matters how the trick was done. The results were marvelous. There had never been such things before.[25]

---

[24]Miguel de Unamuno is similarly critical of Descartes's *cogito:* "The defect of Descartes's *Discourses of Method* lies not in the antecedent methodical doubt; not in his beginning by resolving to doubt everything, a merely intellectual device; but in his resolution to begin by emptying himself of himself, of Descartes, of the real man, the man of flesh and bone, the man who does not want to die, in order that he might be a mere thinker—that is, an abstraction. But the real man returned and thrust himself into philosophy" *(The Tragic Sense of Life,* trans. J. E. Crawford Flitch [New York: Dover, 1954], p. 34). He continues: "The *ego* implicit in this enthymeme, *ego cogito, ergo ego sum,* is an unreal—that is, an ideal—*ego* or I, and its *sum,* its existence, something unreal also. 'I think, therefore I am a thinker'; this being of the 'I am,' which deduced from 'I think,' is merely a knowing; this being is knowledge, but not life. And the primary reality is not that I think, but that I live, for those also live who do not think. Although this living may not be a real living" (p. 35).
[25]Richard Rorty, *Contingency, Irony and Solidarity* (Cambridge: Cambridge University Press, 1989), p. 17.

Not only does thought just happen, it is this thought that creates the self: "the human self is created by the use of a vocabulary."[26] Rorty credits Nietzsche with the notion. Nietzsche, he says, saw that "self-knowledge as self-creation, confronting one's contingency, tracking one's causes home, is identical with the process of inventing a new language—that is, of thinking up some new metaphors."[27]

For Rorty, the creation of the self by language is liberating. It frees people to change themselves and society. The formula is neat: Change the language and you change the self and society. In fact, "changing languages and other social practices may produce human beings of a sort that had never before existed."[28]

It looks as if Nietzsche was prophetic: some have learned "to get along without the little 'it' (which is all that is left of the honest little old ego)."[29] Nietzsche was right to question whether much is accomplished by the *cogito* argument. There may be thinking; there may be a thinker. But what is that thinker? "What is the 'I'"? is still a pointed question. If one begins from the subjective self, one ends by losing any reason for thinking there is a subjective self. The human self has died.

---

[26]Rorty writes, "The temptation to look for criteria is a species of the more general temptation to think of the world, or the human self, as possessing an intrinsic nature, and essence. . . . But if we could ever become reconciled to the idea that most of reality is indifferent to our descriptions of it, and that the human self is created by the use of a vocabulary rather than being adequately or inadequately expressed in a vocabulary, then we should at last have assimilated what was true in the Romantic idea that truth is made rather than found, and that truth is a property of linguistic entities, or sentences" (ibid., p. 7).

[27]Ibid., p. 27. Rorty also credits Wittgenstein with a similar notion, noting that "Wittgenstein's insistence that vocabularies—all vocabularies, even those which contain the words which we take most seriously, the ones essential to our self-descriptions—are human creations, tools for creation of such other human artifacts as poems, utopian societies, scientific theories, and future generations" (Rorty, *Contingency*, p. 53). Rorty's reduction of knowledge to language itself has come under severe criticism; see, for example, Alvin Goldman, *Knowledge in a Social World* (Oxford: Oxford University Press, 1999), pp. 10-12, 26-28; Donald Davidson, "Truth Rehabilitated," in *Rorty and His Critics*, ed. Robert Brandom (Oxford: Blackwell, 2000), pp. 65-74; and Charles Taylor, "Rorty in the Epistemological Tradition," in *Reading Rorty: Critical Responses to "Philosophy and the Mirror of Nature" (and Beyond)*, ed. Alan R. Malachowski (Oxford: Blackwell, 1990), pp. 257-75.

[28]Rorty, *Contingency*, p. 7.

[29]Nietzsche, *Beyond Good and Evil*, p. 214.

REVELATION AS THE FIRST THING

Perhaps the strongest objection to my contention that ontology precedes
epistemology is that I have forgotten that as Christians we get our knowledge about what first things are supposed to be not from human self-reflection but from revelation. As human beings we are finite. We can know nothing about God unless he tells us. This he has done in small part in the
natural order but mainly in Scripture. Revelation—the gift of knowledge
about what we would scarce have any knowledge at all—must necessarily
precede what we understand God to be. So it must come first.

Indeed this is true in terms of the order of knowing. We receive what is
put before us through the general revelation of God in the world and the
special revelation of God in Scripture. But in a worldview the order of being precedes the order of knowing. Before there can be revelation, there
must be something to be revealed and someone or something to reveal it.
Revelation can never be first, as if we or God depended on it. It always depends on God.[30]

It is interesting to see how this plays out in various attempts to construct
a systematic theology. John Calvin begins with the knowledge of God and
ourselves, then quickly argues that it is God who imbues everyone with the
knowledge of his existence so that without special revelation all people
know of God's existence, though that knowledge is inadequate and misleading. Scripture is necessary for a proper knowledge of God. It is God,
however, that is his focus.[31] Calvin, in other words, believes that every human being has a concept of God. In worldview terms, Calvin—though he

---

[30] E. L. Mascall explains this cleverly: "One of the drawbacks of being a mere creature is that
you see everything the wrong way round; you look at things from man's standpoint and not
from God's. The order in which things ultimately exist, the *ordo essendi*, is usually the precise
opposite of the order in which we come to know them, the *ordo cognoscendi*; and this is spe-
cially true of that which is of all beings the most fundamental, namely God himself." As we
grow up we learn about God in our home or community, perhaps even engaging in devo-
tional activity. "The logical order is the reverse of this: God comes first; then Christ, who is
God incarnate in human flesh; and last of all, the faith and devotion of the Church which
Christ founded. And this is, in fact, the order adopted by both the Apostles' and the Nicene
Creeds, which begin with God the Father, then summarize the facts of the Incarnation and
of Redemption, and only at the end mention the inspired Scriptures, the Church and Bap-
tism" (*He Who Is: A Study in Traditional Theism* [London: Libra, 1966], p. 11.
[31] John Calvin *Institutes of the Christian Religion* 1.1-15.

begins with epistemology—quickly shifts the focus to ontology. It is because of who God is that everyone first has an immediate pretheoretical knowledge of his existence and some of his attributes and then, if they are exposed to the Scripture, has special revelation that will clarify and correct their understanding.[32]

Theology of the twentieth and twenty-first centuries, however, is conditioned by the basically hostile environment in which it has been produced and which it seeks to counter. Much of this environment is characterized by the Enlightenment that followed quickly after the work of Descartes and John Locke. Both took their start from epistemological rather than ontological foundations. Descartes, as we have seen, placed his confidence in human reason to find truth, and Locke trusted in the mind's ability to order and perceive with the senses. In both cases, the autonomy of human reason replaced confidence in special revelation or any previous human authority such as Plato or Aristotle, Augustine or Aquinas. As Peter Medawar says, the notion of the *"necessity* of human reason" slowly gave way to "the *sufficiency* of human reason."[33] Thenceforth all intellectually respectable beliefs had to pass the bar of human reason.

Twentieth-century Christian theology has largely accepted the challenge and has attempted in a variety of ways to show how it satisfies this notion of reasonability. Some theologies abandon the traditional Christian distinctives because they do not measure up. Others attempt to show how even the notions that seem most unreasonable to modern people actually are reasonable by the criteria of modern human reason.

Apologists, for example, often argue that the resurrection of Jesus is the most rational explanation of the evidence we have available in the Gospel narratives and that these narratives themselves can be shown by human reason to be historically reliable. There is good reason for such apologists to

---

[32]"That there exists in the human mind, and indeed by natural instinct, some sense of Deity, we hold to be beyond dispute, since God himself, to prevent any man from pretending ignorance, has endued all men with some idea of his Godhead, the memory of which he constantly renews and occasionally enlarges, that all men to a man, being aware that there is a God, and that he is their Maker, may be condemned by their own conscience when they neither worship him nor consecrate their lives to his service" (Calvin *Institutes* 1.3.1).
[33]Peter Medawar, "On 'the Effecting of All Things Possible,'" *The Listener*, October 2, 1969, p. 438.

take this route as a starting point for dialogue with nonbelievers and, as a prologue to the doctrine of God, for believers. Few thoughtful people today will easily grant the authority of the Bible on any topic whatsoever, let alone on the key issues of Christian faith. But apologetics is not the foundation of either theology or Christian faith in general.[34] It is rather the theological and philosophical discipline of showing how the Christian understanding of God and the world is the best explanation we have for what we experience as human beings living in a complex world.

In any case, a Christian worldview is not the same thing as a Christian theology. Both deal with the same or similar issues. A worldview includes a consciousness of a pretheoretical dimension. A theology normally assumes this dimension rather than inquiring in to the nature of its presuppositions.

HERMENEUTICS FIRST

Finally, we return to the addition to worldview analysis made by David Naugle and described in the previous chapter. A worldview, he writes, "is a semiotic system of narrative signs that has a significant influence on the fundamental human activities of reasoning, interpreting, and knowing."[35] In the postmodern world of the early twenty-first century, we might expect that approach to be lifted to the realm of ontology. We might easily imagine that a worldview could be defined primarily in relation to semiotics or hermeneu-

---

[34]Some evangelical apologists do assume that some key aspects of the Christian faith can, for all intents and purposes, be proved or at least adequately defended through human reason. Aquinas's famous five reasons still appear in modern form in Catholic and Protestant apologetics. So do proofs for Jesus' divinity or the resurrection. Still, it seems to me that the most effective apologetic does not start with positive proofs but answers to objections—whatever they are (naturalistic or postmodern)—the most common of which are the problem of evil, the belief in God as arising from psychological or sociological causes, the origin of the orderly universe by a combination of chance and determinism, the evolutionary origin of human beings through natural causes, and the notion of the relativity of all truth claims. When these are disposed of—or before, if possible—attention should be directed to the best evidence for God in any place or time: Jesus himself. The focus should be on Jesus' character, teaching, life, death and resurrection. The idea of this apologetic evangelism is to turn attention to Jesus as the incarnation of God, that is as Being himself. It is the living God who breaks through by being He Who Is. In the final analysis, even if the order of knowing (ordo cognoscendi) in human time precedes the order of being (ordo essendi), He Who Is has already preceded we who are and has done so both in time and in presence.

[35]David Naugle, Worldview: The History of a Concept (Grand Rapids, Mich.: Eerdmans, 2002), p. 253.

tics. If this happened, then ontology would collapse into hermeneutics. "What holds up the world?" the son asks. The postmodern dad would answer, "Meaning holds up the world, Son, just meaning. It's all interpretation. Come, let us interpret."

Then, captured by language not invented by either father or son, both would become victims of language itself. Indeed, in the words of Nietzsche, truth would be "a mobile army of metaphors."[36] The world would then spin off into linguistic space, where "the earth is unchained from the sun" and "strays through an infinite nothing."[37] The world would not so much hang in space as hang on deconstructed language.

Of course, if the father and son were "strong poets" capable of controlling the language that people use, then their linguistic usage would become the definition of reality.[38] There would be no way to test whether their language comported with nonlingustic reality. As Foucault says, "'Truth' is to be understood as a system of ordered procedures for the production, regulation, distribution, circulation, and operation of statements."[39] Their locutions would merely be "pseudointerpretations of an ultimate reality all dressed up in a linguistic power suit."[40]

What counts against putting meaning first is the commonsense notion that *something has to be* before there can be meaning. A worldview certainly can be "expressed in a semiotic system of narrative signs." But it has to be something else first; it is not created by the signs by which it is understood. The pretheoretical categories themselves seem to be universal: *being* and *not-being (is* and *isn't)* are fundamental and carry truth value; that is, they label something that is not just linguistic.

I recall a rabbi a number of years ago who was trying to help a small group of evangelical professors understand what the Jews mean by "the land." He said, and I paraphrase, "The land is not defined by a geopolitical

---

[36]Friedrich Nietzsche, "On Truth and Lie in an Extra-Moral Sense," in *The Portable Nietzsche*, trans. Walter Kaufmann (New York: Viking, 1954), p. 46.
[37]Friedrich Nietzsche, *The Gay Science* 125, in *Portable Nietzsche*, p. 95.
[38]For Richard Rorty's elaboration of Harold Bloom's notion of "strong poet," see Rorty, *Contingency*, pp. 23-42.
[39]Michel Foucault, "Truth and Power," in *The Foucault Reader*, ed. Paul Rabinow (New York: Pantheon, 1984), p. 74.
[40]Naugle, *Worldview*, p. 184.

line on a map. It's material stuff." He bent down as if to pick up a handful of dirt, but we were in a synagogue and he came up empty-handed.

The world has substantiality. Yes, it is also a sign. Evangelicals have missed much of the richness of the biblical worldview when they have dismissed sacramental theology as medieval and misguided. It has taken writers such as C. S. Lewis to bring us back to considering its riches. In *The Great Divorce*, heaven is more substantial than earth, hell less substantial.[41] I think Lewis got it right.

I do not want to miss the substantiality of God by seeing our view of him as a set of signs. Moses asked God, "Show me your glory." Moses was not ready for that yet, and neither are we. But the Logos has been incarnated on earth. He retains his body in heaven (whatever that means).

Naugle gives an example of reading Jesus' life and death in terms of signs:

> It is quite likely that the hostility aimed at Jesus and a primary reason for his crucifixion was that during his ministry he directly and indirectly attacked the sacred symbols of the Second Temple Jewish worldview. Indeed, the semiotic system of his own ministry was extraordinarily provocative, and he virtually reorganized the entire Jewish theological tradition through his proclamation of the mysteries of the kingdom of God.[42]

Yes, one can quite rightly understand Jesus' actions in this way. But it is not the symbols that were at stake. It was the reality the symbols symbolized. It was not God as he really is that was being worshiped. So while Christians recognize the symbolic nature of reality, we also realize the substantiality of that which is symbolized. A postmodern can answer, "It's language all the way down." A Christian ought not.

CONCLUSION

I have taken a long and circuitous way to justify my simple conclusion. But the point is important. Ontology must precede epistemology in worldview formulation. If it does not, we are basing our whole worldview on the fragile structure of the human ego, that is, on the autonomy of human reason, which really means the autonomy of each person's human ego or each

---

[41]C. S. Lewis, *The Great Divorce* (London: Geoffrey Bles, 1946), pp. 27-29.
[42]Naugle, *Worldview*, p. 296.

community's sense of reason. To do this is dangerous. The justification of our worldview must not be autonomous human reason, even if it is reason as represented by the Christian tradition. The biblical priority of Being—God as Being—is replaced with epistemology or, more accurately, hermeneutics. The Christian worldview under these conditions becomes not just modern but postmodern.

Let me simply say it again: Ontology precedes epistemology and hermeneutics—and whatever else there may be.

4

Flesh and Bones
THEORETICAL AND PRETHEORETICAL

*Man is obviously made for thinking. Therein lies his dignity and
his merit; and his whole duty is to think as he ought.*

BLAISE PASCAL, *PENSÉES*

When the boy asks his father about what holds up the world, he is already doing so from a basic worldview. He understands up and down. He sees a model of the solar system in which bodies seem to hang in space.

Within the framework of the boy's worldview, the question is natural. How it is answered, however, may serve to alter or enhance the dimensions of that worldview. Both the worldview that lies behind the boy's question and the more detailed worldview implicit in the father's answer are deeply involved with the society in which the boy and the father live. Their whole discourse is embedded in a worldview community.

There is little argument about the role that social context plays in the formation of one's worldview. How could it be otherwise? Raised in a Hindu family in Poona, India, a child will take on the culture of his or her life situation. This will largely be done unconsciously. Thousands of tiny thoughts and judgments will become the intimate property of the growing child. If there is little contact with a family outside the Hindu religion, there may be rebellion against some aspects of the society, but there will be few options for a young adult to take. If, on the other hand, the Hindu family is living in Downers Grove, Illinois, the growing child will be exposed to a host of living alternatives, a bevy of conflicting faiths and no-faith, a pluralism of influences. Pluralistic cultures give lots of worldview options. Still, some aspects of worldviews are universal. Here we will deal with one of them—the theoretical, pretheoretical and presuppositional nature of worldviews.

From the first elaboration of the notion, analysts have agreed that worldviews are not first *theoretical* but rather *pretheoretical (intuitive)* and/or *presuppositional.* As Wilhelm Dilthey says, "Every worldview is an intuition."[1] That is, the foundational suppositions are those conceptions that we cannot imagine not being characteristic of the world. They are the thoughts we think with when we think anything. David Naugle calls them the "subterranean impressions about the world conceived by an anesthetized yet functioning mind" and "untested, groundless 'substratum' for all inquiry and assertions."[2] For sociologist Karl Mannheim, "worldviews are virtually unconscious phenomena, having risen spontaneously and unintentionally. As deep unformed, germinal entities, they are taken for granted by those who embrace them and yet they are the prime movers in thought and action."[3]

Still, is there no difference between what is signified by these three terms? Is everything that constitutes a worldview totally beyond thoughtful derivation or consideration? That is, is everything in a worldview to be taken intuitively?

As we have seen, we do come to the place where we can no longer give telling reasons for the views we hold. We stand as the father answering his son's question "What holds up the world?" and all we can do is say—or shout—"It's Elephant all the way down." As Ludwig Wittgenstein puts it,

---

[1] Wilhelm Dilthey, quoted in David Naugle, *Worldview: The History of a Concept* (Grand Rapids, Mich.: Eerdmans, 2002), pp. 82-83.

[2] Naugle's summary first of Friedrich Wilhelm Joseph von Schelling's view (ibid., p. 61), then that of Ludwig Wittgenstein (p. 160).

[3] Quoted in ibid., p. 225. Lovejoy does not use the word *worldview,* but his description of the sorts of ideas that intellectual historians should consider sounds very much like those constituting a worldview: "There are, first, implicit or incompletely explicit *assumptions,* or more or less *unconscious mental habits,* operating in the thought of an individual or a generation. It is the beliefs which are so much a matter of course that they are rather tacitly presupposed than formally expressed and argued for, the ways of thinking which seem so natural and inevitable that they are not scrutinized with the eye of logical self-consciousness, that often are most decisive of the character of a philosopher's doctrine, and still oftener of the dominant intellectual tendencies of an age" (A. O. Lovejoy, *The Great Chain of Being: The Study of the History of an Idea* [Cambridge: Harvard University Press, 1933], p. 7).

"If I have exhausted the justifications, I have reached bedrock, and my spade is turned. Then I am inclined to say: 'This is simply what I do.'"[4] We see that final reality is either the material order of the universe itself or something beyond that material order, something or someone supernatural. Even though we have some reason, or even many reasons, for choosing one or the other, our experience in dialogue with others shows us that we cannot *prove* our worldview beyond the shadow of a doubt. And though we may hold our presuppositions consciously and with a confidence approaching certainty, we also know that we could be wrong. After all, we have changed our mind before. Could we not do so again? So our commitment remains at least in part a matter of faith. In short, our worldview at its heart is presuppositional.

But if our worldview is presuppositional, must it also be pretheoretical? That is, must it be so intuited or given to us that we can't think any other than the way we do? I think not. The utterly pretheoretical is that without which we cannot think at all. The presuppositional is that which, though we may be able to give reasons for, we cannot, strictly speaking, prove.[5] Nevertheless we believe so profoundly that we commit ourselves to it and live in accord with it. We cannot do otherwise, for we need it in order to give our life enough meaning to keep going.[6] Finally, the *theoretical* is that which arises from the mind's conscious activity.

PRETHEORETICAL

Let us first examine the utterly pretheoretical. What notions are so basic and so much a part of our mental equipment that if we think at all, we are

---

[4]Ludwig Wittgenstein, *Philosophical Investigations* (Oxford: Blackwell, 1967), sec. 217, quoted by James Olthuis, "On Worldviews," in *Stained Glass: Worldviews and Social Science*, ed. Paul A. Marshall, Sander Griffoen and Richard J. Mouw (Lanham, Md.: University Press of America, 1989), p. 31.

[5]I am aware that there are other ways of defining *presuppositional*. Arthur Holmes notes that a presupposition has also been defined as a "logical prior proposition, as in presuppositionalist apologetics, especially Gordon Clark and Carl Henry's kind of evangelical foundationalism" (personal communication). I want to emphasize not so much the clear intellectual content of this aspect of a worldview as its root in intuition and its function in commitment.

[6]Psychiatrist Armand Nicholi Jr. says, "Evidence exists that the human brain is 'hardwired' (genetically programmed) for belief" (*The Question of God: C. S. Lewis and Sigmund Freud Debate God, Love, Sex and the Meaning of Life* [New York: Free Press, 2002], p. 46).

forced to use them? Aristotle listed ten such categories; among them are substance, quality, quantity, relation, place and time, all of which seem to me to fit this criterion.[7] Descartes thought the notion of truth itself was pre-theoretical, even though he could give it a theoretical definition as "the conformity of thought with its object."[8] It is hard to imagine how we could even begin to think without implicitly using—not thinking about but using—some of these categories.

Two modern cultural anthropologists expand Aristotle's list. Michael Kearney names the categories of "self and the other, relationship, classification, causality, space and time."[9] Robert Redfield lists the self (divided into I and me) and the other (divided into human and nonhuman). The human is further divided into young and old, male and female, us and them; the nonhuman is divided into God and nature. Finally, what Redfield calls "everyman's worldview" includes space and time, birth and death.[10] My guess is that there are many more of these pretheoretical concepts to include, for example, meaning, oughtness, identity and contradiction.

[7] See "category" in *The Cambridge Dictionary of Philosophy* (Cambridge: Cambridge University Press, 1995), p. 108. Pascal lists space, time, motion and number (Blaise Pascal, *Pensées*, trans. A. J. Krailsheimer (Middlesex, U.K.: Penguin, 1966), no. 110, p. 58; Arthur F. Holmes considers the pretheoretical categories in *Contours of a Christian Worldview* (Grand Rapids, Mich.: Eerdmans, 1983), p. 48; and Everett W. Hall examines the truth value implicit in the categories themselves (*Philosophical Systems: A Categorical Analysis* [Chicago: University of Chicago Press, 1960], esp. pp. 1-6, 22-25).

[8] [Truth] seems to be a notion so transcendentally clear that no one could be ignorant of it. . . . There is no way to learn what truth is, if one does not know it by nature. . . . Of course, it is possible to tell the meaning of the word to someone who does not know the language, and tell him that the word *truth*, in the strict sense, denotes the conformity of thought with its object. . . . But we can give no definition of logic which will help anyone discover its nature" (Descartes in a letter to Marin Mersene in 1639, quoted by Stephen Gaukroger, *Descartes: An Intellectual Biography* (Oxford: Clarendon, 1995), p. 327). Descartes is stating what is called the "truth of correspondence." Scholastic philosopher Étienne Gilson further clarifies the concept this way: "To say what is true is to say what is, and to attribute to each thing the very being that it marks. Thus it is the being of a thing which founds its truth; and it is the truth of a thing which underlies the truth of thought" (*A Gilson Reader: Selected Writings of Étienne Gilson* [Garden City, N.Y.: Image, 1957], p. 247). It is unlikely that any other theories of truth—coherence or pragmatic, for example—could be pretheoretical. That very fact may well indicate a certain inadequacy if and when these theories replace the truth of correspondence as the reigning concept.

[9] Michael Kearney, quoted in Naugle, *Worldview*, p. 242.

[10] Robert Redfield, quoted in ibid., p. 246.

In short, the pretheoretical consists of those notions and recognitions of relationships between notions that precede any thought at all. The pretheoretical is what we think with, not what we think about.

Look again at the young boy's first question: "What holds up the world?" Already assumed is the difference between his *self* and the *other* of his father, the *substantial* existence *(being* as opposed to *nonbeing)* of the world in *place* and *time.* These concepts are not questioned. Their specific relationship is at issue, but not the notion of relationship itself. What is utterly pretheoretical is the intellectual context in which the boy's question makes sense.

PRESUPPOSITIONAL

Worldviews, then, include the pretheoretical in their basic character. Still, there are some notions that are difficult to place solely in these pretheoretical categories. Chief among these is the notion of God. Is *God* an innate pretheoretical concept, or does it derive from mental reflection or social or psychological implantation?

Sigmund Freud would, of course, take the latter view. For Freud, God does not exist. The idea, therefore, could not be innate, a result of human beings' being made in the image of God or their receiving some revelation of God from God. The notion of God rather derives from the human need for consolation in a hostile world. It is a human invention. In fact, all religious doctrines are illusions, the result of wish fulfillment.[11]

This does not mean, of course, that the way anyone acquires the notion of God is theoretical. The idea may well be pretheoretical in the sense that it was acquired unconsciously. Religious ideas have "psychical origins": "These which are given out as teachings are not precipitates of experience or end-results of thinking: they are illusions, fulfilments of the oldest, strongest and most urgent wishes of mankind. The secret of their strength lies in the strength of those wishes."[12]

But unlike the notion of space or time or being, God is not a concep-

[11]Sigmund Freud, *The Future of an Illusion,* trans. James Strachey (New York: W. W. Norton, 1961), pp. 30-33—but the entire book is devoted to this issue. See also Nicholi, *Question of God,* pp. 36-56.
[12]Freud, *Future of an Illusion,* p. 30.

tion we must have before we think about God. The idea of God is more like the idea of a king. We can learn about kings without having any preconception of what a king is. So we learn about God from our social context. As Freud says, "Think of the depressing contrast between the radiant intelligence of a healthy child and the feeble intellectual powers of the average adult. I think it would be a very long time before a child who was not influenced began to trouble himself about things in another world."[13]

Thomas Aquinas and John Calvin, on the other hand, take the notion of God to be a direct perception of God's existence, one unmediated by society or psychological need. Aquinas says, "To know that God exists in a general and confused way is implanted in us by nature."[14] Calvin goes further. He says that everyone has a *sensus divinitatis*, a sense of deity:

> That there exists in the human mind, and indeed by natural instinct, some sense of Deity, we hold to be beyond dispute, since God himself, to prevent any man from pretending ignorance, has endued all men with some idea of his Godhead, the memory of which he constantly renews and occasionally enlarges, that all to a man, being aware that there is a God, and that he is their Maker, may be condemned by their own conscience when they neither worship him nor consecrate their lives to his service.[15]

Notice that it is not just God as abstract Being but as Creator that is grasped by the human mind. That would seem to include personhood as well. Whether or not the notion of any God is pretheoretical is itself a worldview matter. Alvin Plantinga is helpful here: "The *sensus divinitatis* is a disposition or set of dispositions to form theistic beliefs in various circumstances, in response to the sorts of conditions or stimuli that trigger the working of this sense of divinity."[16] So triggered by a starry sky, a mag-

[13]Ibid., p. 47.

[14]Thomas Aquinas, "Whether the Existence of God Is Self-Evident: Reply to Objection I," in *Summa Theologica*, 2nd and rev. ed., trans. Fathers of the English Dominican Province (online ed., 2003), <www.newadvent.org/summa/100201.htm>.

[15]John Calvin, *Institutes of the Christian Religion*, trans. Henry Beveridge (London: James Clarke, 1957), p. 43 (1.3.1).

[16]Alvin Plantinga, *Warranted Christian Belief* (New York: Oxford University Press, 2000), p. 173.

nificent mountain, a sense of guilt or any number of other natural stimuli, belief arises. Plantinga says, "I simply find myself with the belief in God."¹⁷ This sense is not so much the conclusion of an argument as an intuitive grasp of an idea or a being who just comes to mind. In this sense, belief in God is like our belief that two plus two equals four. We just "see" that it does.¹⁸

For a Calvinist, and perhaps for other Christians as well, it is a pretheoretical concept; for a consistent naturalist, it is not and cannot be.

But this raises an interesting question. If the Calvinist is right, the naturalist has had, at least at one time, an intuitive grasp of the existence of God. The Calvinist would use as the authority for this Romans 1:18-20:

> The wrath of God is revealed from heaven against all ungodliness and wickedness of those who by their wickedness suppress the truth. For what can be known about God is plain to them, because God has shown it to them. Ever since the creation of the world his eternal power and divine nature, invisible though they are, have been understood and seen through the things he has made.

If, for example, Freud no longer intuits the existence of God, or no longer concludes God's existence from his observation of the world around him, it is because he has suppressed the truth through his own wickedness. According to a Calvinist worldview, then, Freud may presuppose the final reality to be the material world, he may even give reasons for this presupposition, but he is both wrong and responsible for being wrong. He could and should have known better.

Calvin would say that the father's obvious answer to his son's question about what holds up the world is God. It is not a "no brainer," for there are

---

¹⁷Ibid.
¹⁸Following Calvin's lead, it would be easy to see why Descartes thought that his idea of God was something he simply found himself to have and that it must have come from God. Descartes, of course, considered his innate idea to be so clear and distinct and of such a transcendent nature that he couldn't have produced it himself. Calvin is content to observe its origin without making from it a philosophical proof for God's existence, something he would have considered unnecessary (you don't need an argument for the existence of someone whom you know directly). Calvin is more interested in the fact that it leaves human beings with no excuse for their failure to live up to God's requirements.

reasons for the intuition—the existence of the world around us. But confidence in this knowledge of the existence of God goes beyond any argument for it. It is predicated on the God-given human ability to sense God's existence directly. Freud's failure to sense God's existence is due not so much to his intellectual as to his moral failure. The truth is there, not just in front of him (as the phenomena of the world) but in him (as the *sensus divinitatis*). As Pascal so intriguingly said, "The heart has reasons of which reason knows nothing."[19]

Freud the naturalist, on the other hand, attributes belief in God to a psychological need for God. It is something that intelligent people—like Freud—must learn to do without. "Scientific work is the only road which can lead us to a knowledge of reality outside ourselves."[20] The reason Calvin believes in God, Freud would say, is that he has failed to use his intelligence and has succumbed to his feeling of inadequacy. He has imagined what does not exist but what satisfies his inner lack.

The conflict boils down to this: either human beings are made in the image of a God with at least some human characteristics (Calvin), or God is made in the image of human beings (Freud). Arguments for both views depend on the same information. The question is, which is the origin of which—God the origin of human beings or human beings the origin of the concept of God?

If the case were really this simple, then what orients our lives—belief in God or belief in ourselves—would be solely a matter of a coin toss. If neither can refute the other's argument and make a telling case for his own view, then the radical fideists are right. One is reduced to blind choice leading to blind faith.[21] At this point in the argument, however, we ought not concede the case to the radical fideists. It may very well be that the case against Freud and others like him is very strong and that the case for the existence of God can be made with considerable rigor and justifi-

---

[19] Blaise Pascal, *Pensées*, trans. A. J. Krailsheimer (Harmondsworth, U.K.: Penguin, 1966), no. 423, p. 154. Also see no. 110, p. 58.
[20] Freud, *Future of an Illusion*, p. 31.
[21] By "radical fideists" I mean those who believe that there is no rational way to justify one's beliefs; they are primitive and unanalyzable. As one student in Denmark once asked me, "Isn't faith more faith when it can give no reason for what it affirms?" He said he got this idea from Kierkegaard, but I suspect this is a misreading.

cation.[22] But the issue does illustrate the role that presuppositions have in both arguments and in orienting worldviews. (This issue is taken up again in chapter six.)

There is another way to consider the presuppositional nature of the concept of God. Take the first presupposition I identify in *The Universe Next Door* as the Christian worldview answer to the question, What is prime reality—the really real? The Christian answer is God. And who is God?

God is the infinite and personal (triune), transcendent and immanent, omniscient, sovereign and good being who created the universe.[23]

Except for the opening word, none of this answer is pretheoretical. It is, rather, a complex predication about the character of the "really real." It is, in other words, a statement about being itself. God is the really real. God is being itself. But what is being? That is, what does it mean to say God is being? The pretheoretical part of this proposition is the concept of being itself, that is, the innate recognition of the difference between what is and what is not. We don't know being by thinking about what being actually is but by pretheoretically grasping the notion.[24] We intuitively know the difference between that which is and that which is not. There is no more primary concept. We can say that by "being" we mean "that which is," or "isness," but unless we have already grasped the concept, these rewordings mean no more than what the word *being* already means.

Thus all thought about any specific being—ourselves, the world around us, God or the gods—is founded on a pretheoretical given, a concept that we either get or don't get. But this concept is so fundamental that it would

[22]Nicholi makes such a case against Freud (*Question of God*, pp. 36-56). Christian arguments for the existence of God have a very long history. See, for example, Étienne Gilson, *God and Philosophy* (New Haven, Conn.: Yale University Press, 1941); E. L. Mascall, *He Who Is: A Study in Traditional Theism* (London: Libra, 1966); J. P. Moreland, *Scaling the Secular City* (Grand Rapids, Mich.: Baker, 1987); Richard Swinburne, *The Existence of God* (Oxford: Oxford University Press, 1979; Peter Kreeft and Ron Tacelli, "Twenty Arguments for the Existence of God," in *Handbook of Christian Apologetics* (Downers Grove, Ill.: InterVarsity Press, 1994), pp. 47-88; Steven T. Davis, *God, Reason and Theistic Proofs* (Grand Rapids, Mich.: Eerdmans, 1997); and J. P. Moreland and William Lane Craig, *Philosophical Foundations for a Christian Worldview* (Downers Grove, Ill.: InterVarsity Press, 2003), pp. 463-500.
[23]This definition is based on the first two propositions of Christian theism in James W. Sire, *The Universe Next Door*, 3rd ed. (Downers Grove, Ill: InterVarsity Press, 1997), pp. 23-24.
[24]Martin Heidegger's massive *Being and Time* is an attempt to elucidate the concept of being, which, he says, has not been done since the pre-Socratic philosophers.

not be possible for any normally functioning human being not to have it. One does not need to be particularly intelligent. The dullest persons who carry on meaningful conversations already grasp the distinction between being and not being. They may not be able to articulate the notion, but everything they say implies the distinction.

In short, it may be that what is truly pretheoretical is not the idea of God but the concept of being. That is, the concept of God may not be sufficiently primitive to be pretheoretical. It may not necessarily carry definitional content—personal or impersonal, Creator or emanater of the rest of reality, one or many.

If the apostle Paul were to weigh in on this issue, based on what he said in Romans 1:18-20, what would he say? "Eternal power and divine nature": these are the attributes of God that Paul says everyone knows. Surely it is the Christian God—not Allah or Brahman—that Calvin says we know by our *sensus divinitatis*.

Perhaps, however, the apostle does not mean to include as many characteristics as Calvin implies. Calvin holds that God as Maker is intuited, but would he hold that the *sensus divinitatis* gives us access to all the traditional characteristics of the theistic God (infinite and personal [triune], transcendent and immanent, omniscient, sovereign and good)? Except for *good*, these are all theoretical terms; their application to the concept of God can surely be seen as presuppositional, but are they also pretheoretical? How much theoretical content do "eternal power" and "divine nature" contain? If Paul is correct, does the pretheoretical include some theoretical content? I confess, I don't know the answers to these questions. Rather than speculate, as a Christian I am content to leave them unanswered, at least for the moment.[25]

---

[25]Thomas Aquinas and his neoscholastic interpreters, notably Étienne Gilson and E. L. Mascal, would argue that by the light of natural reason it can be shown that God as supreme Being (as the really real) must necessarily exist and that he must have a number of attributes that carry theoretical content. Noting that science cannot answer why there is something rather than nothing, Gilson says that scholastic philosophy can: "To this supreme question, the only conceivable answer is that each and every particular energy, each and every particular existing thing, depends for its existence upon a pure Act of existence. In order to be the ultimate answer to all existential problems, this supreme cause has to be absolute existence. Being absolute, such a cause is self-sufficient; if it creates, its creative act must be free. Since it creates not only being but order, it must be something which at least contains the principle of order

The existence of God is, of course, fundamental to worldview analysis. But what about other key worldview matters? There are some issues that cause our heart to beat faster, our brow to sweat, our psyche to boil, our spirit or soul or self or core of our being—whatever makes me *me*—to sag. If they are not dealt with, they can send us into not just a brown funk but a mental hospital. Take the problem of evil and pain. Why is there so much of it? Why do my friends suffer? And worse, why me too? But the most troubling of these issues is death. What happens to a person at death? I can't believe I will live forever. Death is certain. So what will happen to me?

I am certain that something will happen to me at death. I can fantasize that I will not die, that I will continue to live as I have for the few or many years since my birth, but I cannot be certain which one of several options will be my fate. If I am to lay this question to rest with some sort of answer, it will not be—so it seems to me—because the answer is so certain that I cannot help but accept it. I do not mean that I do not or cannot have some confidence (Lesslie Newbigin would call it "proper confidence") in a specific answer, say, reincarnation, resurrection, extinction or transformation to another state of being.[26] I mean that none of these possibilities are anywhere near as certain as the simple fact that I will cease to live in my present bodily form.

I suggest, therefore, that some aspects of a worldview are presuppositional without being pretheoretical. That is, within the Christian worldview is the notion that at death each human being will continue in existence, eventually being resurrected either to a blissful life with God and his people or to a continued unhappy existence forever separated from God and all that brings joy.

---

known to us in experience, namely, thought. Now an absolute, self-subsisting, and knowing cause is not an It but a He. In short, the first cause [what I have called the really real] is the One in whom the cause of both nature and history coincide, a philosophical God who can also be the God of a religion" (*God and Philosophy*, pp. 139-41). Beyond this, Gilson refuses to go, arguing that for much of our Christian concept of God revelation is necessary. Though Mascall would not say that the notion of God as the "I AM" is a pretheoretical notion, he does believe that this "metaphysic of Exodus" includes by implication a host of characteristics other than simple existence as such: "It draws into unity all the other attributes and operations of God: simplicity, perfection, goodness, infinity, immutability, eternity, unity, his character as Prime Mover, as Uncaused Cause, as Sufficient Reason, as Perfect Pattern and as Final End of all things" (*He Who Is*, p. 13).

[26]Lesslie Newbigin, *Proper Confidence: Faith, Doubt and Certainty in Christian Discipleship* (Grand Rapids, Mich.: Eerdmans, 1995).

Some Christians probably could give little conscious reason to believe this (perhaps they are children and have picked it up from home and church), some could give a number of reasons that they find satisfactory, and some could give sophisticated justifications for their belief. But in the final analysis, the specific Christian concept of life after death, no matter how simple or complex, is a *belief* that is held on *faith*. But, of course, the same is true of naturalists who believe that all personal existence ends at death. Among naturalists who believe in extinction at death there is the same mix of people—some with no conscious reasons, some with some, some with many.

In short, the concept of death itself is pretheoretical—a given. The particular character of death is not. In an analogy suggested by cultural anthropologist Michael Kearney, every worldview has both bones and flesh.[27] I suggest that the bones are pretheoretical, the flesh is presuppositional.

FOUNDATIONS OF THE FOUNDATIONAL

Herman Dooyeweerd gives the presuppositional nature of worldviews a peculiarly theological twist by insisting that at root there are only two fundamental worldviews: the one originating from a ground motive *(grondmotief)* of people converted by God, all others originating from a ground motive of people still bound by sin.[28] In doing this, he seems to be giving a foundation even to the pretheoretical notions I have identified, that is, a sort of subfoundation to what I have been calling a foundation. He locates the origin of human cognition in the central core of each person. If one is converted, one's whole worldview at every level will be radically different from that of one who is not converted. Dooyeweerd writes,

> [A worldview] requires the religious commitment of our selfhood. It has its own attitude of thought. . . . Its view of totality is not *theoretical*, but rather *pretheoretical*. It does not conceive of reality in its abstracted modal aspects of meaning, but rather in typical structures of individuality which are not analyzed in a theoretical way.[29]

---

[27] It is not clear whether this analogy derives from Kearney or Naugle (Naugle, *Worldview*, p. 243).

[28] Ibid., pp. 25-29.

[29] Herman Dooyeweerd, *A New Critique of Theoretical Thought*, trans. David H. Freeman and William S. Young (n.p.: Presbyterian & Reformed, 1969), 1:128.

Dooyeweerd is not easy to understand. As best I can make out, he is saying that the relationship to God of a redeemed and regenerated believer stands at the source of his or her worldview.[30] The converted have a Christian worldview; the unconverted can't even begin to grasp what that worldview might be. To see from a Christian perspective, one must be a Christian. In some Reformed scholars this has reinforced, if not led to, a rejection of any rational apologetic for the Christian faith. The unconverted can in no way grasp the force of a case for Christianity. The gospel is thus only to be proclaimed, not argued for.

What interests me here, however, is Dooyeweerd's location of the source of worldviews in the *pre*-pretheoretical spiritual core of each human being. I have found few worldview analysts who find Dooyeweerd's position to represent reality.[31] The major reason, I think, is that there is such a large overlap between how Christians and non-Christians view reality that Dooyeweerd's radical antithesis between the Christian worldview and all others seems not to describe reality. Both a Christian and a non-Christian see buses coming down the street, and both get out of the way. Both have senses of right and wrong, which often register the same judgment. Moreover, for some of the converted, human reason and rational argument have played an important role in their conversion. C. S. Lewis is a case in point.[32]

There is, however, a curious parallel to Dooyeweerd's notion of ground motive. Kierkegaard in an early work described a conversion experience that leads to the formation of a "life-view"[33]:

If we now ask how a life-view comes about, then we reply that for him who does not permit his life to fizzle out, but who tries insofar as possible to balance the individual events in life—that for him there must necessarily come

---

[30] See Jacob Klapwijk, "On Worldviews and Philosophy," in *Stained Glass: Worldviews and Social Science*, ed. Paul A. Marshall, Sander Griffoen and Richard J. Mouw (Lanham, Md.: University Press of America, 1989), pp. 46-48, 50-52.

[31] One such is Jacob Klapwijk (see esp. ibid., p. 45).

[32] C. S. Lewis, *Surprised by Joy: The Shape of My Early Life* (London: Geoffrey Bles, 1955); David C. Downing, *The Most Reluctant Convert: C. S. Lewis's Journey to Faith* (Downers Grove, Ill.: InterVarsity Press, 2002).

[33] Kierkegaard "preferred the term *livsanskuelse* (lifeview) over *verdensanskuelse* (worldview), since it captured the existential character of his philosophy, though on a few occasions he uses the terms synonymously" (Naugle, *Worldview*, p. 75).

> a moment of unusual illumination about life, without his needing in any way
> to have understood all the possible particulars to the subsequent understand-
> ing of which he has in the meantime [come to have] the key: I say, there must
> come a time when . . . life is understood backwards through the Idea.[34]

In other words, conversion—"a *kairos* moment in one's experience"[35]—
precedes the formation of a worldview, which one understands retrospec-
tively. It is discovered by reflection, not produced by imagination or rational
thought. In later works Kiekegaard expands on this notion, seeing, for example, the religious life-view as incorporating and redeeming the aesthetic
and ethical modes.[36]

AN ONTOLOGICAL PERSPECTIVE

All of the ruminations above focus on epistemological issues. What if we
step back and remind ourselves that it is ontology that precedes epistemology? Before something can be rightly theoretical, pretheoretical or presuppositional, that which constitutes it must exist. That is, if the theoretical,
pretheoretical and presuppositional represent reality more or less accurately, that reality must be there to be represented. From a realist ontological perspective, the object of knowledge controls the way knowledge of the
object will be able to be apprehended.

Material objects present themselves to us in their materiality, and if we
know them, we know them in relationship to what they are. A city bus is
known as a city bus because it is a city bus. If I am in the middle of a busy
street, I will want to know that bus for what it is. The bus may have no intention of making itself known to me, but it does so by its very nature as a
specific material object. God too presents himself to us as he is, but unlike
a material object, when he does present himself to us, he does so intention-
ally and in whatever mode he wishes. That is, God is in total control of what
his creatures will be able to know and will know about him. He reveals. We
perceive. He gives. We receive.

Looked at this way, the focus is not on the role of human experience in
apprehending God, not on our grasping after the knowledge of God, not on

---

[34]Søren Kierkegaard, quoted in Naugle, *Worldview*, pp. 76-77.
[35]Naugle, *Worldview*, p. 77.
[36]Ibid., pp. 73-82.

our search for God. God is already there. The focus is on our receiving from him the gift of the knowledge of his constant, immanent presence. The Scripture gives us numerous examples of God's revealing presence. As the opening of Hebrews summarizes, "Long ago God spoke to our ancestors in many and various ways by the prophets, but in these last days he has spoken to us by a Son, whom he appointed heir of all things, through whom he also created the worlds" (Heb 1:1-2).

The connection between one's worldview and one's religious experiences may well be forever lost in the mystery of transcendence itself. From our finite point of view, the infinite is impenetrable. The infinite, if it is personal, can reveal itself to us; we can never discover its character on our own. Within the Christian understanding, the pretheoretical—whether it be the categories of our thought (like *substance, being, self*) or our intuition of God—will always be beyond analysis. We may learn about the pretheoretical from Scripture, but it will be because God has revealed what he has wanted to reveal. Speculation—our only other recourse—will almost surely be misleading, as it was for Freud.

I conclude this reflection on the pretheoretical, presuppositional and intuitive, then, by observing that all three are characteristic of worldviews, they overlap and cannot always be distinguished, and they form the basis of our theoretical thought and profoundly influence our practical action.

5

Rational System, Way of Life and Master Story

The Christian tradition of rationality takes as its starting point not any alleged self-evident truths. Its starting point is events in which God made himself known to men and women in particular circumstances—to Abraham and Moses, to the long succession of prophets, and to the first apostles and witnesses who saw and heard and touched the incarnate Word of God himself, Jesus of Nazareth.

LESSLIE NEWBIGIN, *THE GOSPEL IN A PLURALIST SOCIETY*

This book began with a story, a story that led to a series of questions and answers. Then the story itself largely dropped away from our attention, and we focused on the questions and their answers. In other words, the discussion so far has proceeded as if a worldview were a set of propositions or beliefs that serve as answers to a systematic set of questions. This certainly is how I understood the notion of worldview as I wrote *The Universe Next Door*. I still believe that this is a useful way to define the concept, but I have become aware that it both overemphasizes the systematic nature of worldviews and misses some other important aspects. So what is inadequate? And what is missing? Those are the subjects of this chapter.

First, to what extent is a worldview a systematic set of propositions? Second, if a worldview is the answers to a set of questions, what are the questions?

Third, if it is something else or something more, what is that? Could it be a way of life, or perhaps a master story into which we see our lives fitting?

A SYSTEMATIC SET OF PROPOSITIONS

One clear expression of the notion of a worldview is Sigmund Freud's equation of *worldview* with a complete, tacked-down, systematic, virtually certain philosophy of life:

> In my opinion . . . a *Weltanschauung* is an intellectual construction which solves all the problems of existence uniformly on the basis of one overriding hypothesis, which, accordingly, leaves no question unanswered and in which everything that interests us finds its fixed place.[1]

On this definition, psychoanalysis is not a worldview but instead relies on the worldview of modern science, which asserts that "there are no sources of knowledge of the universe other than the intellectual working-over of carefully scrutinized observations—in other words, what we call research—and alongside of it no knowledge derived from revelation, intuition or divination."[2] Freud himself has no interest in formulating a specific worldview. He is content with what today is called *scientism*, the notion that materialistic (naturalistic) science can answer all the questions that can be answered and that these are the only questions that need to be answered.

The building of worldviews themselves, Freud says, can be "left to philosophers, who avowedly find it impossible to make their journey through life without a Baedeker [travel guide] of that kind to give them information on every subject."[3] The irony of his readily adopting scientism as a worldview while ridiculing those who would thoughtfully examine it and all other worldviews is quite lost on him. And so, were Freud alive to see it, would be the irony of the current assessment of the accuracy of Freud's psychoanalytic theories. For, as intellectual historian Peter Watson says, "Freudianism has never found unequivocal empirical support, and the very idea of a systematic unconscious, and the tripartite di-

---

[1] Sigmund Freud, "The Question of a *Weltanschauung*," in *The Standard Edition of the Complete Psychological Works of Sigmund Freud*, trans. James Strachey with Anna Freud, 24 vols. (London: Hogarth Press, 1953-1974), 22:158.
[2] Ibid., p. 159.
[3] Freud, "Inhibitions, Symptoms and Anxiety," in *The Standard Edition*, 20:96.

vision of the mind into the id, ego, and superego, has seemed increasingly far-fetched. . . . [In short], the dominant intellectual presence of our century was, for the most part, wrong."[4] Even scientism now condemns psychoanalysis.

Though there are others who think of a worldview as a complete system or a "theory of everything,"[5] this notion has not been at the center of the present book. A worldview needs to be neither conscious nor basically consistent. It need not answer every question that can be raised, only those relevant to each person's life situation. In *The Universe Next Door* I do identify a series of somewhat consistent worldviews—Christian theism, naturalism, pantheism, for example—but these are ideal types outlined for heuristic purposes, not because anyone, including myself, holds precisely the worldview as described. Everyone's worldview is a bit different from that of everyone else; moreover, worldviews can change subtly and unconsciously over the years. Still, everyone has a worldview.

If Freud's definition were to stand, we would have to find another term for the concept a host of worldview analysts are talking about. Nonetheless, Freud's conception deserves mention. It illustrates an important thesis of both Naugle and the present book: the concept of worldview is worldview

---

[4]Peter Watson, *The Modern Mind: An Intellectual History of the 20th Century* (New York: HarperCollins, 2001), pp. 759-60.
[5]Philosopher Theodore Plantinga insists on using the term *worldview* to mean a "theory of everything." So his critique and ultimate rejection of *worldview* for Christian analysis is not of much value in assessing its actual usefulness when defined as something much less than a "theory of everything." Any given person's worldview need not address all possible issues, only those relevant to his or her personal life situation. The more general, abstract worldview need only provide enough general conceptions to allow extrapolations to be made in areas that may later emerge historically. The Christian worldview in the sixteenth century did not have or need an explicit way of dealing with nuclear war or human cloning. But it already had the basic foundation for dealing with such issues. Moreover, Plantinga's implicit notion that a worldview must be unified and consistent keeps him from seeing that while a single person has only one worldview, it might look to an outsider as if he had more than one because he does not seem to act or speak from a single point of view. Plantinga likewise makes too much of the *view* part of *worldview*, seeing the notion as visual and not paying enough attention to what people who use the term say they mean by it. His objection to those who talk of "a Christian worldview" as opposed to "the Christian worldview" is moot, if one uses the term to mean something other than a complete, final and true theory of everything. See "David Naugle and the Quest for a Theory of Everything," *Myodicy*, no. 17, December 2002 <www.redeemer.on.ca/~tplanti/m/MCD.HTM>.

dependent. The worldview of scientism fits well with Freud's conception of what a worldview is.

Still, there is some connection between Freud's conception and the one dominating this book. Freud says, "A worldview leaves no question unanswered." I say that every worldview will answer a few very basic questions, often with utter self-assurance, sometimes with great reticence. But what are the right questions? What are the ones a worldview must in some way address?

THE RIGHT QUESTIONS

A number of analysts define worldviews in relation to a series of questions. Sometimes these questions are given as if they were only illustrative, as if others could or should be added. In *The Universe Next Door* I tried to list most if not all of the key ones. Having seen other lists, however, I have wondered if I succeeded or if I miscast some of them.

I have listed my own questions before, but for reference, here they are again:

1. What is prime reality—the really real?

2. What is the nature of external reality, that is, the world around us?

3. What is a human being?

4. What happens to persons at death?

5. Why is it possible to know anything at all?

6. How do we know what is right and wrong?

7. What is the meaning of human history?

The first four questions are ontological; question 5 is epistemological; question 6 is ethical; and question 7 is a return to ontology. These questions are as broad and inclusive as I could make them at the time. They attempt to get at the foundations of all our human thoughts and actions—with one exception.

As an English literature teacher who had written his dissertation on a topic involving aesthetics, I knew from the first that I had omitted one worldview question: What is the beautiful? I left the question unasked and unanswered for two reasons. First, it is almost impossible to answer simply or clearly, let alone definitively, even within an otherwise well-developed worldview. Second, for most people, aesthetics is not a conscious existential concern. People like what they like and dislike what they dislike, and that's all there is to popular aesthetics. Moreover, in the Protestant Christian world, my own subculture, it is largely ignored except for the very small artistic community and those people with an insatiable and well-developed appreciation of the beauty of cultural objects.

But are there other questions that are missing? Could the questions be better framed? A brief survey provides more than perspective; it suggests a missing dimension.

Wilhelm Dilthey writes,

> The riddle of existence . . . is always bound up organically with that of the world itself and with the question of what I am supposed to do in this world, why I am in it, and how my life in it will end. Where did I come from? Why do I exist? What will become of me? This is the most general question of all questions and the one that most concerns me.[6]

These questions are subsumed under my questions 3, 4 and 7, though they are prefaced here by a more existential tone.

Anthropologist Robert Redfield (1897-1958) defines a worldview as "the way a people characteristically look outward upon the universe." He "articulates four sets of questions based on these ubiquitous worldview themes: What is confronted? What is the nature of the not-man? What is man called upon to do? What is the source of the orderliness of things?"[7] These questions are subsumed under my questions 1, 2 and 3.

James Orr notes that two types of causes—speculative and practical—are involved in the formation of worldviews. Both "lie deep in the constitution of human nature." On the one hand, we want a comprehensive theoretical understanding of the "origin, purpose, and destiny" of the universe and our lives. But we also want a practical understanding of these issues so that we can properly order our lives. So we ask these questions:

---

[6]Wilhelm Dilthey, *Gesammelte Schriften*, 8:99, quoted in David Naugle, *Worldview: The History of a Concept* (Grand Rapids, Mich.: Eerdmans, 2002), p. 83.
[7]Robert Redfield, *The Primitive Worldview and Its Transformation*, p. 85, quoted in Naugle, *Worldview*, p. 245.

Is the constitution of things good or evil? By what ultimate principles ought man to be guided in the framing and ordering of his life? What is the true end of existence? What rational justification does the nature of things afford for the higher sentiments of duty and religion? If it be the case, as the Agnostic affirms, that light absolutely fails us on questions of origin, cause and end, what conception of life remains? Or, assuming that no higher origin for life and mind can be postulated than matter and force, what revision is necessary of current conceptions of private morality and social duty?[8]

Orr's questions arise from his desire not just to understand the Christian worldview but to do so in a hostile intellectual environment. The Christian worldview has an apologetic task to perform. What follows in *The Christian View of God and the World* is an elaborate set of answers to the questions he asks.

Theologians Brian Walsh and Richard Middleton select three themes from Christianity as central to the Christian worldview: the doctrine of creation, the fall of humanity into sin, and transformation through Christian redemption. These biblical motifs answer the four fundamental worldview questions that are at the heart of every worldview:

(1) *Who am I?* Or, what is the nature, task and purpose of human beings?
(2) *Where am I?* Or, what is the nature of the world and universe I live in?
(3) *What's wrong?* Or, what is the basic problem or obstacle that keeps me from attaining fulfillment? In other words, how do I understand evil? And
(4) *What is the remedy?* Or, how is it possible to overcome this hindrance to my fulfillment? In other words, how do I find salvation?[9]

[8]James Orr, *The Christian View of God and the World* (Grand Rapids, Mich.: Eerdmans, 1954), p. 7. Orr quotes as well from Thomas H. Huxley, *Man's Place in the Universe*: "The question of questions for mankind, the problem which underlies all others, and is more deeply interesting than any other, is the ascertainment of the place which man occupies in nature, and of his relation to the universe of things. Whence our race has come, what are the limits of our power over nature, and of nature's power over us? to what goal we are tending? are the problems which present themselves anew, and with undiminished interest, to every man born in the world?" (p. 7n).
[9]Brian J. Walsh and J. Richard Middleton, *The Transforming Vision: Shaping a Christian World View* (Downers Grove, Ill.: InterVarsity Press, 1984), p. 35. Almost identical to Walsh and Middleton's questions are those of David Dockery: "Where did we come from? Who are we? What has gone wrong with the world? What solution can be offered to fix it?" (David Dockery, "Shaping a Christian Worldview," in *Shaping a Christian Worldview*, ed. David Dockery

The questions as stated here begin not with God or external reality but with the individual self. Nonetheless, as Walsh and Middleton further explain them, it is obvious that God (or ultimate reality) is central to their concerns and that who we are is to be answered in communal, not individualistic, terms. The first three are covered in my questions 1 and 3. But their question 3 also singles out one particularly complex issue for any theistic worldview to deal with—the problem of evil. This issue is a part of the answers given to my worldview questions 3 and 7, but it is not a focus in my system.

Redfield is the sole analyst who clearly begins with ontological issues. His first two and his fourth questions are ontological; the third is ethical. With Dilthey, Orr, and to some extent, Walsh and Middleton, the questions focus on existential concerns. They are all about us. While the answers will involve God and nature, the emphasis is practical. What are the implications for us as human beings looking for a satisfying life? Orr includes in his larger list of questions all the issues raised by others, with perhaps the exception of the remedy for the human condition. Only Orr addresses epistemology, but while he does so, he does not ask how one can know that any of one's answers to the other questions are true or even credible (my question 5). Rather, he assumes that answers to epistemological questions will be able to be given "rational justification."

It appears, therefore, that my seven questions are in fact fairly comprehensive. They include in some way the essence of all the questions that others have formulated. This should not be surprising, since the questions address ontology, epistemology and ethics. What else besides aesthetics is left?

What is missing from my seven questions is not content but existential relevance. True, the fourth question ("What happens to persons at death?") is existential, but the others are not. We turn, then, to look at worldview as a way of life that is bound up with seeing one's own life as a part of a master story, a metanarrative.

[Nashville: Broadman & Holman, 2002], p. 3). Likewise Charles Colson echoes Walsh and Middleton with, "Where did we come from and who are we *(creation)?* What has gone wrong with the world *(fall)?* And what can we do to fix it *(redemption)?*" (Charles Colson and Nancy Pearcey, *How Now Shall We Live?* [Wheaton, Ill.: Tyndale House, 1999], p. 14).

WORLDVIEW AS A WAY OF LIFE

While worldviews have been overwhelmingly detected and expounded using intellectual categories, from the first there has been a recognition that
they are inextricably tied to lived experience and behavior. "Every true
world-view is an intuition which emerges from the *standing in-the-middle-
of-life*" (emphasis added).[10] People are looking for "stability," says Dilthey,
and so they both create and rest in a conception of reality that allows them
to live and move and have their being in a universe that is not totally hostile.[11] And while Kuyper is aware of the German word *Weltanschauung*,
translated as "worldview" in English, in his own English-language lectures
on Calvinism he uses, depending on the context, either "life-system" or
"life and world view."[12]

Walsh and Middleton follow the same focus on lived reality: "World
views are best understood as we see them incarnated, fleshed out in actual
ways of life. They are not systems of thought, like theologies or philoso-
phies. Rather, worldviews are perceptual frameworks." This can be seen
from two angles, one diagnostic or analytic, the other life-foundational.
From a diagnostic angle, we can assess whether we ourselves (or anyone
else) hold a particular worldview by observing how we or others act. Worldviews are "ways of seeing," Walsh and Middleton say, and add, "If we want
to understand what people see, or how well people see, we need to watch
how they walk. If they bump into certain objects or stumble over them,
then we can assume that they are blind to them. Conversely, their eyes may
not only see but dwell on certain other objects."[13]

Walsh and Middleton then illustrate this by describing how four fam-
ilies in four different cultures from the same social classes care for their
babies. Each set of actions illustrates a different "life form" or worldview. "A world view is never merely a vision *of* life. It is always a vision
for life."[14]

---

[10] Dilthey, quoted by Naugle, *Worldview*, pp. 82-83.
[11] Ibid., p. 86.
[12] Abraham Kuyper, *Lectures on Calvinism* (Grand Rapids, Mich.: Eerdmans, 1931), p. 11.
[13] Walsh and Middleton, *Transforming Vision*, p. 17.
[14] Ibid., p. 31. The positive and practical implications of living out one's worldview are brilliantly
explained and illustrated in Steve Garber, *The Fabric of Faithfulness: Weaving Together Belief
and Behavior During the University Years* (Downers Grove, Ill.: 1996), esp. pp. 108-24.

The relationship between *of* life and *for* life is two-way, symbiotic. How we view life affects the life we live; it governs both the unconscious actions we engage in and the actions we ponder before acting. That means that our individual worldview is somewhat fluid. Sometimes, due to a crisis or a sudden insight or realization, our worldview shifts so much that *conversion* is the best term to describe the change. In noncrisis, ordinary interaction with the world outside the self, our worldview varies only slightly.

Sometimes, however, our worldview varies in one direction so slightly and so persistently that we suddenly realize that we have changed our orientation without knowing it. For example, I was raised in a church where I learned the rudiments of dispensational theology. Ten years after high school, I was surprised to discover that I had lost most of my peculiarly dispensational worldview and had become basically Reformed. This is a change within the limits of Christianity itself, but, of course, some gradual changes of worldview end up being much more radical. Small, gradual changes can also lead to conversion.

In their second book, *Truth Is Stranger Than It Used to Be*, Middleton and Walsh plumb more deeply the connection between culture and worldview. Still working with the four questions in *The Transforming Vision*, they examine the difference between the modern and postmodern worldviews. Note their answers to their first two worldview questions.

They take the story of Columbus as one narrative locus for modernity. "*Where are we?* We are in the New World, the lost Eden which has now been found. . . . We are in a world that is ripe for the taking and that offers up its riches to those who know how to exploit them. *Who are we?* We are the conquistadors . . . who have taken this wild land inhabited by savages and tamed it."[15] Postmodernity gives radically different answers. "*Where are we?* We are in a pluralistic world of our own construction. *Who are we?* We are Legion [like the madman in Mark 5 who was inhabited by many demons]."[16]

Dilthey and Middleton and Walsh are clearly correct in their judgment.

---

[15]Richard Middleton and Brian J. Walsh, *Truth Is Stranger Than It Used to Be* (Downers Grove, Ill.: InterVarsity Press, 1995), p. 11.
[16]Ibid., p. 56.

Every operative worldview directs action. This aspect, the practical, lived reality of worldviews, is missing from the definition given in the first three editions of *The Universe Next Door* and needs to be included in any revision.

WORLDVIEW AS MASTER STORY

All worldviews have at least some operative concept of the passing of time and its relation to both human and nonhuman reality. Folklore, myth and literature around the world from the ancient past to the present tell stories that put present human reality in the larger context of universal cosmic and human meaning.[17] They act as orienting patterns. In short, they function as worldviews or parts of worldviews.[18] The worldviews of Buddhism, Hinduism and primal religion are embedded and embodied in stories. While few of these sets of stories may be easily tied together in one master story, one metanarrative, nevertheless these are the stories by which societies interpret the universe and life around them.

While the Enlightenment with its progeny, modernity, has tried to reject such stories as primitive superstition, happily replacing them with universal rational, propositional knowledge, that very attempt is story-ful. Naturalism itself relies on evolution (cosmic, geological, biological, cultural and psychological) to explain the universe in general, what we are as human beings and how we got this way. Postmodernism tends also to be historicist, seeing the whole of how we understand ourselves and God (if any) to be bound up with the ebbs and flows of culture and societal change.[19]

Both in the works of most Christian worldview analysts—such as James Orr, James Olthuis, Arthur Holmes and Ronald Nash—and my own *Universe*

---

[17]For a seminal work in noting the link between narrative style and worldview content, see Erich Auerbach, *Mimesis: The Representation of Reality in Western Literature* (Garden City, N.J.: Doubleday/Anchor, 1953), pp. 1-20.

[18]David Lyle Jeffrey says, "The structure of formative narratives . . . bespeaks a *Weltanschauung*, a worldview" ("Masterplot and Meaning in Biblical Narrative," in *Houses of Interpretation: Reading Scripture, Reading Culture* [Waco, Tex.: Baylor University Press, 2003], p. 16). Jeffrey then outlines the master stories of Islam, Christianity, and ancient Greece and Rome, but the entire essay (pp. 15-38) is a rich commentary on themes dealt with in this section.

[19]As much as postmodern scholars try to reject all metanarratives, they illustrate a metanarrative by their rejection. For the notion that all metanarratives are suspect is itself an overarching "story" about other overarching stories. See Jean-François Lyotard, *The Postmodern Condition: A Report on Knowledge*, trans. Geoff Bennington and Brian Massumi (Minneapolis: University of Minnesota Press, 1979).

Next Door, worldview is first described in intellectual terms, such as "system of beliefs," "set of presuppositions" or "conceptual scheme." I want now to ask whether this is quite accurate. Does it not miss an important element in how people actually think and act? Isn't a *story* involved in how we make the decisions of belief and behavior that constitute our lives? Would it be better to consider a worldview as the *story* we live by? Certainly Naugle agrees here: "The most fundamental stories associated with a *Weltanschauung*—those closest to its metaphysical and ethical epicenter—possess a kind of finality as the ultimate interpretation of reality in all its multifaceted aspects."[20]

Perhaps the easiest way to see that this might be the case is to examine the Christian worldview. I have argued that the Christian worldview begins with ontology—an abstract concept, but soon ontology becomes lodged in story form. The ancient Apostles' Creed demonstrates this:

> I believe in God, the Father Almighty,
>> Maker of heaven and earth,
>> and in Jesus Christ, his only Son, our Lord.

Only the first line is utterly ontological. The second line brings in action, and while it does not take a position on whether creation was in or out of time, it recognizes God as origin of the earth. It is the fourth line that roots the Christian worldview in story:

> Who was conceived of the Holy Spirit,
>> born of the Virgin Mary,
>> suffered under Pontius Pilate,
>> was crucified, died, and was buried.
>
> He descended into hell.
>> The third day he rose again from the dead.

There is no reason to quote further. The remainder of the creed is steeped in story. None of it, really, is as abstract as most lists of beliefs one assents to before joining a specific church, and certainly it is less abstract than the formulation I offered in *The Universe Next Door.*

I began this section by commenting on the Apostles' Creed because it is

[20]Naugle, *Worldview,* pp. 302-3.

an early attempt by the developing church to encapsulate the essence of the Christian faith. When one turns to the Bible itself, the ground of all Christian theologies—Protestant, Catholic, Orthodox—the element of story is even stronger. Most of the Bible is story, and all of it is embedded in story—a history, a story of events that really happened (not just-so stories, or likely stories, or myths). The narratives recount events that bear an inherent meaning that is unfolded throughout subsequent commentary by "Scripture" writers, many of them identified as prophets or special religious authorities. Meaning—worldview—is transmitted by these narratives.

One interesting attempt to encapsulate the story nature of the Old Testament is that of James Orr:

> What are the main characteristics of this Old Testament conception? At its root is the idea of a holy, spiritual, self-revealing God, the free Creator of the world, and its continual Preserver. The correlative to this, and springing out of it, is the idea of man as a being made in God's image, and capable of moral relations and spiritual fellowship with his Maker; but who, through sin, has turned aside from the end of his creation, and stands in need of redemption. In the heart of the history, we have the idea of a Divine purpose, working itself out through the calling of a special nation, for the ultimate benefit and blessing of mankind. God's providential rule extends over all creatures and events, and embraces all peoples of the earth, near and remote. In view of the sin and corruption that have overspread the world, His dealings with Israel in particular are preparative to the introduction of a better economy, in which the grace already partially exhibited will be fully revealed. The end is the establishment of a kingdom of God under the rule of the Messiah, in which all national limitations will be removed, the Spirit be poured forth, and Jehovah will become the God of the whole earth. God will make a new covenant with His people and will write His laws by His Spirit in their hearts. Under this happy reign the final triumph of righteousness over sin will be accomplished, and death and all other evils will be abolished. Here is a very remarkable "Weltanschauung," the presence of which at all in the pages of the Hebrew Scriptures is a fact of no ordinary significance. In the comparative history of religions, it stands quite unique. Speculations on the world and its origin are seen growing up in the schools of philosophy; but on the ground of religion there is nothing to compare with this.[21]

---

[21]Orr, *Christian View*, p. 14.

This description blends the theoretical—God as Creator, humankind as made in God's image—with the narrative. They are inextricably intertwined. Nonetheless, Orr's elaboration of the Old Testament worldview is highly intellectual, probably much more so than the worldview of the ordinary Jew living in Old Testament times. Still, its general outline would have been found in minds and hearts of most of the Hebrew community. Orr, of course, identifies the Old Testament worldview from the standpoint of his own place in history. His is the view of a Reformed theologian living at the end of the nineteenth century and attempting to counter the impact of Enlightenment (modern) alternatives to Christian faith. While there is a great deal of objectivity to his description—that is, description that reflects the character of the actual reality being described—there is also a subjectivity reflecting Orr's overall apologetic aim. One can see this easily by comparing Orr's description of the Old Testament worldview with that of Middleton and Walsh.

Writing almost a hundred years after Orr, Middleton and Walsh face a radically different cultural situation. They grew up in an era when the Enlightenment or modern worldview was in serious decline. Their context is postmodernism. Postmodernism has charged that both the Enlightenment modernism and Christianity are "totalizing metanarratives"; by the stories they tell and the conceptions of reality they hold, both constrain human self-understanding and act as oppressive narratives, privileging one class of people over another.

Middleton and Walsh, then, counter this charge by presenting the Old Testament (and later the New Testament) worldview as narratives of freedom.

> It is our contention that the Bible, as the normative, canonical, founding Christian story, works ultimately *against* totalization. It is able to do this because it contains two identifiable counterideological dimensions or antitotalizing factors. . . . The first of these dimensions consists in *a radical sensitivity to suffering* that pervades the biblical narrative from the exodus to the cross. The second consists in the rooting of the story in *God's overarching creational intent*, that delegitimates any narrow, partisan use of the story.[22]

---

[22]Middleton and Walsh, *Truth Is Stranger*, p. 87.

The story of Israel in the Hebrew Scriptures is not a story only for the Hebrews. "Israel is called to be the particular, historically conditioned means of mediating a universal story of the healing of the world."[23] The New Testament is even more explicit about the universal nature of Israel's story: "As Paul makes clear, the story to which Jesus brings resolution is not simply Israel's story, but the story of the world, read precisely through the lens of Israel's story."[24]

Walsh and Middleton's retelling of the metanarrative that incorporates the biblical stories of the Old and New Testament is set explicitly in the overlapping horizons first of the Bible and second of the world at the end of the twentieth century. Answering the four key questions (Who am I? Where am I? What's wrong? What is the remedy?), they express a Christian worldview that is immediately relevant to thoughtful people today. That is, it is both a vision *of* life and a vision *for* life.

Of course, in the first three editions of *The Universe Next Door* I too retell the biblical story, following the standard sequence of creation, fall, redemption and glorification. Such is the pattern of most retellings of the biblical narrative, as it is of Orr and also Middleton and Walsh. But again there is a difference. In my account the narrative is held at a distance, more like the "news from nowhere" than like the narrative of a participant, which, of course, I am and all other human beings are.

Perhaps it is Lesslie Newbigin, calling on the insights of Michael Polanyi, who is the most helpful in conveying the existential relevance of seeing worldviews as narratives. His explanations have long held an important place in my own grasp of the Christian faith, not its content but its existential dimension. "The dogma, the thing given for our acceptance in faith, is not a set of timeless propositions: it is a story."[25] That story comes to us through Scripture. The Bible sets before us, he says,

> a vision of cosmic history from the creation of the world to its consummation,
> of the nations which make up the one human family, and —of course —of
> one nation chosen to be the bearer of the meaning of history for the sake of

---

[23]Ibid., p. 101.
[24]Ibid., p. 106.
[25]Lesslie Newbigin, *The Gospel in a Pluralist Society* (Grand Rapids, Mich.: Eerdmans, 1989), p. 12.

all, and of one man called to be the bearer of that meaning for that nation. The Bible is universal history.[26]

When we accept this story in the fashion God has intended, we do so not just as intellectual assent. We do not just believe it at a distance. We are to *indwell* it as if it were our own story, because it actually is. "The Christian community is invited to *indwell* the story, *tacitly* aware of it as shaping the way we understand, but *focally* attending to the world we live in so that we are able confidently, though not infallibly, to increase our understanding of it and our ability to cope with it."[27]

To indwell a story is to live so much within its framework that we are not so conscious of the story as of what the story allows us to see.[28] Indwelling is like using a telescope. When we look through a telescope, we see things that we cannot see with the naked eye, but we do not "see" the telescope. Rather we *indwell* the instrument in order to do what we could not otherwise do, to see things we otherwise could not see. As a scientist's probe reveals "what's there," so the biblical story reveals what's there on the other side of the story—the kingdom of God and its conflict with the kingdom of this world: "The important thing in the use of the Bible is not to understand the text but to understand the world *through* the text."[29] As our hands, eyes, five senses are extensions of ourselves in contact with the world, so the biblical narrative puts us in contact with the way God, the world and we really are.

As I have been maintaining throughout this book, it is understanding the way things *really are* that is most important. Ontology precedes epistemology. Ontology precedes ethics. Who and what is there directs how we are to behave toward what is there.

"We *indwell* our language, our concepts, our whole plausibility structure [our operative worldview]," says Newbigin. To multiply the metaphors, our worldview becomes our "reading glasses," our "telescope," our "place to stand" to view reality, the hub of our world, the heart of our selves. As Naugle says, "The heart of the matter is that worldview is a matter of the heart."[30]

---

[26]Ibid., p. 89.
[27]Ibid., p. 38.
[28]See ibid., pp. 27-38, 46, 97-98.
[29]Ibid., p. 98.
[30]Naugle, *Worldview*, p. 269.

CONCLUSION

My work is cut out for me now. Substantive changes need to be made in the definition of *worldview* that I presented in chapter one. The concept needs to be widened, not so much to add new questions as to expand the context to include lived reality. Worldview must incorporate the elements that caused the naturalist Dilthey to speak of "standing *in-the-middle-of-life*" with worldviews springing "from the totality of human psychological existence: intellectually in the cognition of reality, affectively in the appraisal of life, and volitionally in the active performance of the will."[31] Kuyper even refused to use the word *worldview*, preferring instead "life system" and "life and world view."[32] We must take that refusal into account.

Redefining *worldview* will be the task of chapter seven. First, we must consider the relationship between an individual's and a society's or culture's worldviews.

---

[31]Quoted in ibid., p. 88.
[32]Kuyper, *Lectures on Calvinism*, p. 11.

6

Worldviews
PUBLIC AND PRIVATE

*Three degrees of latitude upset the whole of jurisprudence and the
meridian determines what is true. . . . It's a funny sort of justice
whose limits are marked by a river; true on this side of the Pyrenees,
false on the other.*

BLAISE PASCAL, *PENSÉES*

Our discussion so far has assumed that worldviews have both a private
and a public dimension. That is, they are both specific commitments held
by individuals and sets of assumptions that characterize a specific community, historical era or entire culture. But we have not yet considered the relationship between them. A second and closely related question is whether
worldviews are representations of objective reality or only subjective frameworks that determine what is perceived and how it is understood. Both of
these issues will be addressed in this chapter.

PUBLIC AND PRIVATE

Everyone has a worldview. Whether we know it or not, we all operate from
a set of assumptions about the world that remain to a large measure hidden
in the unconscious recesses of our mind. That worldview is private.

I wake up in the morning, not asking myself who I am or where I am. I
am immediately aware of a whole host of perceptions that my mind orders
into the recognition that it's morning: I'm home, I'm crawling out of bed.
In this immediate awareness I do not consciously ask or answer, *What is the*

really real? or, *How do I know I am home?* or, *How can I tell the difference between right and wrong?* Rather, my unconscious mind is using a network of presumptions about how to interpret for the conscious mind what is going on. In some way all of the basic worldview questions are being answered by the way I am acting and behaving.

After I have gone through the daily routines of becoming publicly presentable, I may well deal consciously with one or more these questions, especially if I engage in Bible reading and prayer. The notion of the really real will become conscious. I may even sense the presence of this really real. Later, at work, my answers to the worldview questions will come into play over and over as I decide as an editor, say, which manuscripts to recommend for publication, which words, sentences and ideas to tweak and polish or challenge the author on, how I will respond to an artist's cover design or an assistant's request for a more powerful computer. There will be no time during the day or night, not even in my dreams, when my worldview will not be an integral part of who I am. It will be so much a part of what is uniquely me that there will be no other worldview in the universe that is identical to my own. One's worldview is a matter of the heart. If King Louis XIV could say in arrogance, "Je suis l'état," I could almost say in a cockeyed, multilingual, humbler way, "Je suis meine Weltanschauung."

If worldviews are so private and unique, how can we speak of them as public? How can they characterize a community or even a culture? One reason is not hard to see. We are both individuals and members of the human family. Some things about our worldview are common not just to our immediate family, community, nation or century but to the whole of the human race throughout time and space. Among these are the categories noted in chapter three, things like being, time, relation, quantity. Then there are those presuppositions that we hold in common with our broad Western culture: for example, that every individual of any social class is of equal value, or that our senses give us a fairly accurate indication of where we are in time and space. Some presuppositions we hold in common with our fellow religionists. Every human being is in the image of God, say, for Christians. Some presuppositions are common within our nation, community, family. Into this last class falls such a notion as that the people who live in our neighborhood are not to be trusted. As each societal unit becomes smaller, the common presuppositions become more specific and more detailed but, of course, are held by fewer and fewer people. Finally, one's own worldview embodies some elements that are utterly unique.

All this is obvious. What is not so obvious is how the distinctive worldview of an individual influences, or is influenced by, the common worldview of a community. For an insight into this complex phenomenon we can turn to the sociologists of knowledge, among whom I have found Peter Berger and Thomas Luckmann to be the most helpful. "Everyday life," they say, "presents itself as a reality interpreted by men and subjectively meaningful to them as a coherent world."¹ It is the world as interpreted by people that interests the sociology of knowledge.

In fact, according to Berger and Luckmann, the object of their study is the world human beings construct in symbiotic relationship with each other and the natural world around them. They are interested, then, in "the social construction of reality," and what gets constructed is what they call a *world*. This concept seems almost identical to what I have been calling a *worldview*, but Berger and Luckmann shy away from using that term because it smacks too much of philosophy. Moreover, they do not pretend to study reality as it is but reality as it is understood, and that is a socially constructed reality. Take their understanding of the concept of human nature:

> It is an ethnological commonplace that the ways of becoming and being human are as numerous as man's cultures. Humanness is socio-culturally variable. In other words, there is no human nature in the sense of a biologically fixed substratum determining the variability of socio-cultural formations. There is only human nature in the sense of anthropological constants . . . that delimit and permit man's socio-cultural formations.²

What this means in worldview terms is that each culture or society's understanding of what it is to be human rests on only a few common characteristics—pretheoretical givens—and is largely constructed by that society

---

¹Peter L. Berger and Thomas Luckmann, *The Social Construction of Reality* (New York: Anchor, 1967), p. 19.
²Ibid., p. 49.

as it lives within its material context.[3] "While it is possible to say that man has a nature, it is more significant to say that man constructs his own nature, or more simply, that man produces himself."[4]

Berger and Luckmann continue at great length to explain the complex way human self-consciousness and knowledge relate to nature and to the social world. They conclude simply,

> Man is biologically predestined to construct and to inhabit a world with others. This world becomes for him the dominant and definitive reality. Its limits are set by nature. In the dialectic between nature and the socially constructed world the human organism itself is transformed. In this same dialectic man produces reality and thereby produces himself.[5]

How well these social constructions of reality comport with what reality actually is Berger and Luckmann do not say. They are doing a sociological study of what passes for knowledge in a society; they are not doing philosophy or even worldview analysis. So we should not jump to the conclusion that they are taking a philosophic position on what the really real or external reality really is. They are rather pointing out how ideas of what the really real is are mutually embodied in the mind and heart of individuals and in the surrounding society and larger culture. Their point is that the connection between the public and the private is symbiotic. "Men *together* produce a human environment, with the totality of its socio-cultural and psychological formations. . . . *Homo sapiens* is always, and in the same measure, *homo socius*."[6]

WORLDVIEWS AS IDEAL TYPES

There is a second way that worldviews are public. When we refer to *the* Christian worldview—or naturalism, deism or pantheism, for example—we are acknowledging that there are more or less consistent and

---

[3]Berger and Luckmann work within the common boundaries of academic sociology; as such, they assume a methodological naturalism and never consider the possibility of a spiritual reality. The causes leading to any human world, that is, any given social construction of reality, include only those that are natural. If people construct a world with God, gods, goddesses or spirits, that is a result of human action in a social context; revelation as an objective phenomenon cannot be considered a factor.

[4]Berger and Luckmann, *Social Construction*, p. 49.

[5]Ibid., p. 183.

[6]Ibid., p. 51.

coherent systems of grasping reality that characterize whole societies or historical periods. These systems can be expressed in a series of propositions or stories that, while not necessarily held in exactly the same way by any single individual within that society, are generally characteristic of most people in that society.

It is also appropriate to speak of the worldview underlying a particular academic discipline or theories in an academic discipline or a profession. In academic psychology, for example, there are—or have been—both behavioral and cognitive psychology. Both are generally undergirded by naturalism, but there is enough difference at a basic level that one could draw a distinction between them at an almost worldview level. Skinnerian behaviorism, for example, assumes that there is no "inner person" or "soul" or "mind"; all there is is a "bundle of behavioral characteristics." Rejecting that view, cognitive psychology assumes the existence of mind or soul or inner person who as an agent can act outside the nexus of mechanical cause and effect. So within the basically naturalistic worldview, two contrary notions can be found. In Christian theism, too, various Christians take a variety of stances regarding predestination and free will. Calvinists and Arminians alike have basically Christian worldviews.

Some critics of worldview thinking find this pluralism within worldviews distressing, as if the notion of worldview itself were made useless or suspect by such pluralism. If within the notion of worldview one cannot distinguish the true one from those that are false, they seem to be saying, Christians who are after the truth should abandon worldview thinking altogether. But the very notion that worldview thinking is useless as a tool in the search for truth or misleading in the hands of a genuine Christian is itself worldview dependent.[8] Every declaration about worldviews is

[7]Peter Levine writes and quotes Jürgen Habermas, "All individuals who belong to a single age or culture share a common and contingent shape of consciousness, conceptual scheme, epistemic foundation, 'form of life,' 'life-world,' 'practice,' 'linguistically mediated interaction,' 'language game,' 'convention,' 'cultural background,' 'tradition,' 'effective history,' or what have you . . ." (*Nietzsche and the Modern Crisis of the Humanities* (Albany: State University of New York Press, 1995), p. 45.

[8]Philosopher Gregory A. Clark argues to this effect in "The Nature of Conversion: How the Rhetoric of Worldview Philosophy Can Betray Evangelicals," in *The Nature of Confession: Evangelicals and Liberals in Conversation*, ed. Timothy R. Phillips and Dennis Okholm (Downers Grove, Ill.: InterVarsity Press, 1996), pp. 201-18.

based on a worldview.[9] A worldview is simply inescapable.

PLAUSIBILITY STRUCTURE

Perhaps of more significance is the role the public embodiment of a world-view plays in supporting or undermining the unique and private worldview of each individual. To signal the importance of this fact, sociologists of knowledge have given us a special term. As we have seen, they are wary of using a term with roots in the history of philosophy. So they talk about *plausibility structures*. A plausibility structure is the web of beliefs that are so embedded in the minds and hearts of the bulk of a society that people hold them either unconsciously or so firmly that they never think to ask if they are true. In short, a plausibility structure is the worldview of a society, the heart of a society. The society can be of any size—for example, a small Amish community, an academic discipline like anthropology, or a whole nation or group of nations.

One of the main functions of a plausibility structure is to provide the background of beliefs that make arguments easy or hard to accept. If you ask me how to drive from Downers Grove to Westmont in Illinois, I could say, "Take Ogden Avenue east; it's the next suburb." If you ask me how I know, I could give a variety of answers. For example,

- "I have lived in Downers for thirty years."
- "I've looked it up on a map."
- "I read it in the Bible."
- "I dreamed it last night."

Only the first two of those fit the plausibility structure of most people living in the modern world. Even those who believe the Bible would not accept the third reason. They do not believe the Bible answers such questions. Even a New Ager would find the fourth answer bizarre.

---

[9]David Naugle (*Worldview: The History of a Concept* [Grand Rapids, Mich.: Eerdmans, 2002], p. 335) quotes Carl F. H. Henry: "But scholars who deplore the notion of a Christian world view are not immune to sponsoring covertly or promoting an alternative world view while professing to purge Christianity of supposed non-Christian commitments. While Barth dismisses every world view as intellectual barbarism, he has a world view of his own, inconsistent though it may be" (see Carl F. H. Henry, "Fortunes of the Christian World View," *Trinity Journal*, n.s., 19 [1998]: 163-76).

But let us say you ask me how a person gets to heaven. When I reply, "You have to believe in Jesus," you have a further question: "How do you know this?" In this case only the third answer would have a chance of being acceptable, and even it would be acceptable only among those holding a generally Christian worldview. In fact, giving that answer in a religion class in many secular universities would put you on the margin, for the Bible as an authority for anything is not a part of the typical university plausibility structure.

From the standpoint of the sociology of knowledge (as understood by Berger and Luckmann), what we human beings take to be the real nature of reality, including religious reality, is "constructed and maintained through empirically available social processes. Any particular religious world will present itself to consciousness as reality only to the extent that its appropriate plausibility structure is kept in existence."[10] If, for example, one's community is largely Catholic, this religious view will "simply be taken for granted." If the community becomes religiously pluralistic, that is, "if the plausibility structure is weakened," then it will become easier and easier to doubt the truth of Catholicism. "What was previously taken for granted as self-evident reality may now only be reached by a deliberate act of 'faith,' which by definition will have to overcome doubts that keep lurking in the background."[11]

I once heard the British biologist Richard Dawkins, author of *The Blind Watchmaker*, lecture on the nature of science as an enterprise at DePauw University, a liberal arts college in Indiana. He compared the notion of science that is largely accepted by the scientific community with the notions of science that appear in the pages of the British tabloids and that of astrology. During a question-and-answer session, I asked him why he did not compare "normal" science with the notion of "design science" as held by biologist Michael Behe and described in his book *Darwin's Black Box*. His response was telling.

"Well, Michael Behe believes in God," he said. In that audience of some fifty people, mostly college professors, he did not need to say any more. In *The Blind Watchmaker* Dawkins makes clear that science is predicated on

---

[10] Peter Berger, *The Sacred Canopy: Elements of a Sociological Theory of Religion* (New York: Doubleday/Anchor, 1967), p. 150.

[11] Ibid.

completely naturalistic assumptions.[12] Evolutionary science shows that one does not have to invoke God as an explanation for the changes in the biosphere that have brought about the biological complexity we observe today—including human beings. Besides, science is science, not religion. It must never allow nonnatural factors to play a part in explaining anything one observes in nature. In fact, evolutionary science has made it possible, Dawkins has written, for him to be a "fulfilled atheist."

While no one else in the lecture hall might have said quite that, most of the audience of academic professionals would hold that God plays no role in science. When Dawkins accused Behe of believing in God, he needed to say nothing more. He had proved his point. The university plausibility structure provided a complete justification for Dawkins's rejection of design science.

After a slight dramatic pause, however, as he waited for his audience to mentally assent to his wisdom in omitting to mention design science as worthy of consideration (while astrology and the tabloids were worthy), he added, "And besides, Michael Behe is lazy. He should be trying to find the factors leading to the complexity of biological structures instead of attributing these structures to nonnatural factors."

When I pointed out that his answer was an *argumentum ad hominem*, using the pretentious Latin rather than the ordinary English phrase "poisoning the well" or "name calling," he hesitated a bit and then said, "Yes," but then went further in stating just how lazy a scientist Behe is. My question had raised the issue whether natural causes can actually explain complex biological structures. He never addressed that.

A man in the audience then said, "I wonder if you know how difficult it is to teach science in the United States. People keep wanting us to teach *creationism*." Thus did a red herring get dragged across the issue. For this had nothing whatsoever to do with my question. But in the exchange between Dawkins and myself, Dawkins had clearly come out on top.

Worldviews become plausibility structures by their adoption by a society or a segment of society (here, the academic community). When one's individual worldview is identical to that of one's society, there is no need for further proof that the worldview is true.

---

[12]Richard Dawkins, *The Blind Watchmaker* (New York: W. W. Norton, 1986).

In some communities—like the scientific community in most universities—the plausibility structure is relatively detailed and single, or at least dominant. But in a pluralist society such as that in most of Europe and North America, the plausibility structure will be little more than a flimsy scaffold. Made up of a host of different large and small religious and secular communities, it has little binding power. The worldviews of one's next-door neighbors may be as different as those that separated Marco Polo from Genghis Khan or Columbus from the Native Americans.

In the United States, for example, pluralism no longer means that some of us are Baptists and others Methodists, or some of us are Protestants and others Catholics. It now means that our next-door neighbors may be Rastafarians on one side and purely secular, nonreligious folk on the other. Down the block they are building a Hindu temple, and across town a mosque. Our hairdresser may be meditating each morning for twenty minutes on a seemingly meaningless mantra; our grocer sits in a yoga position for a half-hour each evening; our boss takes New Age management training from the Forum. Meanwhile, our churchgoing friends tell us they wonder about reincarnation, and some of them seek out a form of alternative medicine that implies that each of us is totally responsible for our own health, that we both make ourselves sick and have the power to make ourselves well. Everywhere we turn, we find someone with a view different from ours—each one contending that he or she is free to hold this view and is quite content to let us continue to believe whatever we want. As Leon Wieseltier, literary editor of *The New Republic*, puts it,

> Pluralism, after all, is premised not only on difference, but on the proximity of difference: another way to live is never out of mind in America, because it is never out of sight. The sidewalks are crowded with incommensurabilities. You live and work and play with people for whom your view of the world is nonsense, or worse.[13]

Increasing worldview pluralism has over the past forty years fostered the devastation of a plausibility structure that enabled easy belief in any of the

---

[13]Leon Wieseltier, "The Trouble with Multiculturalism," review of *Dictatorship of Virtue: Multiculturalism and the Battle for America's Future*, by Richard Bernstein, *New York Times Book Review*, October 23, 1994, p. 11.

formerly operative worldviews. The only unity that remains is the general agreement that anyone can believe anything at all: one claim to truth is as valid as any other. In popular parlance, what's true for you doesn't have to be true for me. Truth itself is seen to be either multiple and contradictory or not possible at all. The public nature of our current worldview has so impinged on the private character of any specific worldview that that private worldview no longer gives meaning and purpose to one's life. "We live in a pluralist world" becomes "we live in a relativist world."

OBJECTIVE AND SUBJECTIVE

The course of my argument has now moved from the relationship between the public and private nature of worldviews to the struggle between their objective and subjective character. Given the private nature of worldviews, can they really be objective? Are they not always so subjective, so much *my* view or *your* view or even, sociologically speaking, *our* view (plausibility structure) that they are utterly unreliable? Is not the language system we use to think and communicate forever separate from the supposed reality about which we speak? This latter is, as we have seen, one of the main themes of postmodernism.

Despite the anguish that might well accompany this question as it is batted around by the mind, the answer, I think, is clear. As Karl Barth once said in rejecting natural theology, "Nein!" No, it is not necessary to abandon the notion that we can know something about what really is.

If we begin our intellectual quest demanding the kind of certainty Descartes sought, if we assume that the first issue to resolve is how I can know anything at all, we will, I believe, eventually be led either to nihilism or to utter relativism (also a form of nihilism).[4]

Nor will we get any help from the sociology of knowledge as conceived by Berger and Luckmann. Such a sociology is not equipped to answer epistemological questions. It is an empirical science that observes the phenomena of knowledge, not the objects of knowledge. Its own "object of knowledge" is knowledge as such. In an appendix to *The Sacred Canopy* Berger makes this clear:

---

[4]Helmut Thielicke would call it "ciphered nihilism." See his *Nihilism*, trans. John W. Doberstein (London: Routledge & Kegan Paul, 1961), pp. 30-40, 63-65.

No theological, or for that matter anti-theological implications are to be sought anywhere in the argument. . . . Questions raised within the frame of reference of an empirical discipline . . . are not susceptible to answers coming out of the frame of reference of a non-empirical and normative discipline, just as the reverse procedure is inadmissible.[15]

If Berger is correct, what is to be learned about what Berger calls "worlds" and I call "worldviews" is limited. We can draw no conclusions whatsoever about whether any worldview represents the truth about what is really there. Ontological questions cannot be answered. Neither can epistemological questions.

Sociological theory . . . will always view religion *sub specie temporis*, thus of necessity leaving open the question whether and how it might *also* be viewed *sub specie aeternatatis*. Thus sociological theory must, by its own logic, view religion as a human projection, and by the same logic can have nothing to say about the possibility that this projection may refer to something other than the being of its projector.[16]

All we can learn is how worldviews in their public and private dimensions function in relation to social context. This is not everything we would like to know, but it is not nothing. It gives us a keen insight into the subjective and social aspect of worldviews.[17]

There is, however, another way to look at the possibility of objective knowledge. We do not need to begin our intellectual journey with the question of how we know. If we begin instead with what is there, there is way to justify holding that our worldviews have both a subjective and an objective dimension. If the really real is the biblical God, it is possible that at least some of what we think we know is actually, objectively true. I have tried to explain how this is so in chapter two of *The Universe Next Door*. Basically the argument is this: If God, the all-knowing knower of all things, made us in his image, we can be the sometimes-knowing knowers of some things.

---

[15]Berger, *Sacred Canopy*, p. 179.
[16]Ibid., p. 180.
[17]Berger (ibid., pp. 163, 182) makes an interesting attempt to show how in a "world of socio-historical relativity" one might arrive at an " 'Archimedean point' from which to make cognitively valid statements about religious matters." He is especially interested in the moves to do so made by Karl Barth and Dietrich Bonhoeffer.

Even though we are alienated from our Maker, he has never left us without some capacity to know, and he has graciously redeemed us and is transforming us so that now, though we "see through a glass darkly," we will one day see him face to face.[18]

Of course such a set of presuppositions are not self-evidently true, but if they are true, then objective knowledge is possible. When an ontology focused on the nature of God (and the nature of humanity as created in his image) precedes epistemology, intellectual justification of such an ontology is possible.[19] Alvin Plantinga, for example, explains how belief in God can have "three varieties of positive epistemic status": justification, rationality and warrant. If it is in fact the case that human beings are all endowed with a *sensus divinitatis* that allows them to directly sense the existence of God, then no other justification for their belief is necessary. One's belief in God is, as Plantinga puts it, properly basic. The fact of God's existence (ontology) and the fact of the *sensus divinitatis* (ontology) precede and undergird the objective knowledge (epistemology) of the theistic God, a "God Who Is There," as Francis Schaeffer puts it.[20] Plantinga goes on to explain how such epistemic status applies to the whole range of the biblical worldview.[21]

Traditional Christians in general are not about to give up the idea of objective truth. I do not think I speak only for myself when I say that every fiber of my being cries out for a worldview that is not just my own story, my own set of propositions, my own interpretation of life, but one that is universally, objectively true, one in which the really real is the God Who Is

---

[18]I have explained in far more detail how it is that Christians are justified in believing in the objective truth of the Christian worldview in *The Discipleship of the Mind* (Downers Grove, Ill.: InterVarsity Press, 1990), pp. 77-113, and *Why Should Anyone Believe Anything at All?* (Downers Grove, Ill.: InterVarsity Press, 1994).

[19]Gregory A. Clark argues that Christian worldview thinkers recognize they can no longer argue that the Christian worldview is true in the sense that there is a "correspondence between a worldview and reality. For this reason, they flee to a different definition of truth; truth is now 'coherence'" ("The Nature of Conversion," p. 208). I know of no evidence that this charge is true. But I do know that this is not the position taken in the present book or in *The Universe Next Door*. The coherence of a worldview is an important test of its truth; it is not what *truth* means.

[20]Alvin Plantinga, *Warranted Christian Belief* (New York: Oxford University Press, 2000), pp. 167-98.

[21]Ibid., pp. 241-89.

There, and in which human beings are truly made in his image and capable of knowing at least some of "the way things actually are." The Bible assumes that this sort of knowledge is possible and that it is the major vehicle by which we can know what is the case, not just about the world but about this God Who Is There.

"All men by nature desire to know," said Aristotle. Yes, and in a postmodern world we have to add, All of us desire to know the truth, not just a story constructed by ourselves—each of us as individuals, some of us as communities or all of us as human beings. And there is at least one worldview that shows how that is possible, one that can be as intimate for each of us as it can be universal with all of us. We find this worldview laid out in more detail than any of us can comprehend in the Bible. It is indeed a deeply satisfying worldview that is both public and private, both subjective and objective.

7

Worldview

A REFINED DEFINITION

When we accept a certain set of pre-suppositions and use them
as our interpretative framework, we may be said to dwell in them as
we do in our own body.

MICHAEL POLANYI, *PERSONAL KNOWLEDGE*

It is time to draw together the threads of this argument into a final definition of *worldview*. This will not be a definition that tries to incorporate all
the characteristics of all worldview definitions. That is impossible, for the
very concept of worldview is itself worldview dependent. Modern optimis-
tic naturalists, scientists especially, think of worldviews as self-evident assumptions that allow almost certain knowledge of material reality. Post-
Kantian idealists think of worldviews as innate mental structures through
which we order and understand the phenomena of our lives. Postmodernists are likely to see worldviews as linguistic structures by which we construct our world and come to control it. Likewise, a Christian definition of
worldview will depend on its prior commitment to the objective reality of
the infinite-personal God who has created an intelligible cosmos.

But this perspectival nature of worldviews does not commit Christians to
relativism. Pluralism — the side-by-side existence of worldviews that are at
least partially contradictory — is not relativism. Truth as classically understood among the Hebrews as well as the Greeks, the ancients as well as the
moderns, is not relative. Truth as *the way things are* or the accurate representation in language of *the way things are* precludes relativism. The question is not whether there *is* a way things are. That insight is pretheoretical.

The question is what Descartes meant when he considered truth to be one of the categories. Truth, as "the conformity of thought with its object," he said, "seems to be a notion so transcendentally clear that no one could be ignorant of it."[1] Alvin Plantinga notes, "Thomas Reid and others point out that the idea of *truth*, as a relation between beliefs and the world, is part of our native noetic equipment."[2]

My definition of *worldview*, therefore, will necessarily assume that we hold our worldview to be the truth of the matter. If that is so, then the alternative definitions will be false in whatever way they contradict our own when our own is actually true. Of course, we could be wrong or partially wrong. But in a world where there is order, where chaos is not universal, where things are not "every which way," there is indeed a *way things are*.

Still, the history of worldview teaches us a great deal about the character of worldviews. My own refined definition of *worldview* owes much to that history, as I will point out in what follows.

WORLDVIEW: A REFINED DEFINITION, PART 1

The refined definition of *worldview* has two parts—a basic ontological definition and a list of questions that generate the presuppositions that characterize any specific worldview.

> A worldview is a commitment, a fundamental orientation of the heart, that can be expressed as a story or in a set of presuppositions (assumptions which may be true, partially true or entirely false) which we hold (consciously or subconsciously, consistently or inconsistently) about the basic constitution of reality, and that provides the foundation on which we live and move and have our being.

This succinct definition needs to be unpacked. Each phrase represents a specific characteristic that deserves more elaborate comment.

Worldview as commitment. Selecting this phrase—"a worldview is a commitment"—has for me been the hardest part of refining the concept. The primary reason for this is that it makes an ontological claim. That is, it

---

[1] René Descartes, 1639 letter to Marin Mersene, quoted by Stephen Gaukroger, *Descartes: An Intellectual Biography* (Oxford: Clarendon, 1995), p. 327.
[2] Alvin Plantinga, *Warranted Christian Belief* (New York: Oxford University Press, 2000), p. 216.

tries to identify precisely what a worldview *is*. To see the significance of this claim that a worldview is a commitment, notice what is not claimed.

First, a worldview is not fundamentally a set of propositions or a web of beliefs. That is, it is not first and foremost a matter of the intellect. Nor is it fundamentally a matter of language or a semiotic system of narrative signs. The intellect is surely involved, and language is present as a tool of the intellect, but the essence of a worldview lies deep in the inner recesses of the human self. It is a matter of the soul and is represented more as a spiritual orientation, or perhaps disposition, than as a matter of mind alone.

> For God alone my soul waits in silence;
> > from him comes my salvation.
> He alone is my rock and my salvation,
> > my fortress; I shall never be shaken. (Ps 62:1-2)

It is not the biblical God alone, however, who can be seen as one's rock and salvation. For William Ernest Henley (1849-1903), it was his autonomous human self. In "Invictus," a poem read by schoolchildren to illustrate, if not teach, self-reliance, Henley declares in ringing words,

> I am the master of my fate;
> I am the captain of my soul.

These sorts of affirmations represent profound dispositions or commitments of the central core of the whole person.

Second, a worldview is a commitment but not one that is necessarily the result of a conscious decision. We are committed when we act toward an end even when we are unaware of our motives or the goals toward which our actions tend. Worldviews are a matter of the heart.

Worldview as a fundamental orientation of the heart. This notion would be easier to grasp if the word *heart* bore in today's world the weight it bears in Scripture. As David Naugle has so well pointed out, the biblical concept of the heart is far richer than our common parlance would have it. Today we think of the heart as the seat of the emotions (especially tender, sympathetic emotions) and perhaps the will. But it rarely includes the mind. The biblical concept, however, includes the notions of wisdom (Prov 2:10), emotion (Ex 4:14; Jn 14:1), desire and will (1 Chron 29:18), spirituality (Acts 8:21), and intellect (Rom 1:21).[3] In short, and in biblical terms, the heart is "the central defining element of the human person."[4] That is, a worldview is situated in the self—the central operating chamber of every human being. It is from this heart that all one's thoughts and actions proceed.

The phrase "fundamental orientation" likewise bears unpacking. At its root a worldview is pretheoretical, below the conscious mind. It directs the conscious mind from a region not normally accessed by the conscious mind. It is not that the conscious mind cannot think about a worldview and its pretheoretical character. Presumably we are doing that now. It is that normally we do not do this. Rather we think *with* our worldview and *because of* our worldview, not *about* our worldview. People who go through a crisis of belief or have a peculiar bent for philosophic thinking may think about their worldview much of the time. Others, however, may never even become aware of their own worldview, let alone ponder it.

The worldview analyst who best captures this characteristic is Herman Dooyeweerd with his concept of religious "ground motive." As we saw in chapter two, Dooyeweerd identifies two ground motives: "One is born of the spirit or holiness, and the other of the of the spirit of apostasy."[5] That is, a ground motive is a spiritual orientation, the result of a commitment either to the living God of the Bible or to his archenemy. Dooyeweerd sees these ground motives as prior to any worldview.[6] I am, rather, incorporating his concept of ground motive into my definition of *worldview*. In my estimation, simply by being alive in the world, everyone makes and lives out of a religious commitment. The character of that commitment controls the entire character and direction of one's life. This commitment is usually subconscious, but it can be made conscious by self-reflection. Worldview analysis itself can aid us in becoming more conscious of what that commitment has

[3]See David Naugle's extended description of the biblical concept of heart in *Worldview: The History of a Concept* (Grand Rapids, Mich.: Eerdmans, 2002), pp. 267-74. The NRSV translates *kardia* as "mind"; the NIV translates it as "heart."
[4]Ibid., p. 266. John H. Kok calls it "your innermost being, the gut of yourself, the deepest center of your existence, the source of your thoughts, feelings and actions" (*Patterns of the Western Mind*, 2nd ed. [Sioux Center, Iowa: Dordt College Press, 1998], p. 190).
[5]Herman Dooyeweerd, quoted in Naugle, *Worldview*, p. 28.
[6]Herman Dooyeweerd, *A New Critique of Theoretical Thought*, trans. David H. Freeman and William S. Young (n.p.: Presbyterian & Reformed, 1969), 1:128.

been, is now and may become through further reflection and decision.[7]

One philosopher who is well aware of his worldview and how it functions as a foundation for his further theorizing is John Searle. In his lucid study of consciousness, Searle is well aware that his rejection of any notion of a transcendent being is important:

> Given what we know about the details of the world . . . [e.g., matters of chemistry, physics and biology], this world view [naturalism] is not an option. It is not simply up for grabs along with a lot of competing world views. Our problem is not that somehow we have failed to come up with convincing proof of the existence of God or that the hypothesis of an afterlife remains in serious doubt, it is rather that in our deepest reflections we cannot take such options seriously. When we encounter people who claim to believe such things, we may envy them the comfort and security they claim to derive from these beliefs, but at bottom we remain convinced that either they have not heard the news or they are in the grip of faith. . . . And once you accept our world view the only obstacle to granting consciousness its status as a biological feature of organisms is the outmoded dualistic/materialistic assumption that the "mental" character of consciousness makes it impossible for it to be a "physical" property.[8]

What Searle does not seem to understand is, first, that his conviction that there is no god, no transcendent, is as much a matter of faith as is the conviction of a theist that there is such a god, and second, that a Christian may have evidence for this conviction that is equally valid and convincing. Of course, as we saw above with Richard Dawkins, Searle is not the only

---

[7]I did not write the above pages on commitment and heart in order to address Gregory A. Clark's notion that worldview rhetoric "betrays" Christians by keeping them from properly understanding conversion or having a genuine grasp of what it means for Jesus to be "the truth." Still, I think they do so, not so much by disagreeing with Clark's critique of what he understands to be a Christian worldview but by shifting the core notion of worldview from an abstract system of propositions to a fundamental orientation of the heart. See Clark, "The Nature of Conversion: How the Rhetoric of Worldview Philosophy Can Betray Evangelicals," in *The Nature of Confession: Evangelicals & Liberals in Conversation*, ed. Timothy Phillips and Dennis Okholm (Downers Grove, Ill.: InterVarsity Press, 1996), esp. pp. 211-18.

[8]John Searle, *The Rediscovery of the Mind* (Cambridge, Mass.: MIT Press, 1992), pp. 90-91. Searle reflects on responses to a lecture he gave in India. His audience had objected to his materialistic approach by noting that "they personally had existed in their earlier lives as frogs or elephants, etc.": "Given what I know about how the world works, I could not regard their views as serious candidates for truth" (p. 91).

scholar to rely on a plausibility structure to lend credence to an otherwise tendentious argument.[9]

Expressed as a story or in a set of presuppositions. A worldview is not a story or a set of presuppositions, but it can be expressed in those ways. When I reflect on where I and the whole of the human race have come from or where my life or humanity itself is headed, my worldview is being expressed as a story. Naturalism, with its pattern of big bang; evolution of the cosmos; formation of the galaxies, suns and planets; the appearance of life on earth and its eventual disappearance as the universe runs down, is a master story. Nihilism is a master story, perhaps a tale told by an idiot full of sound and fury, signifying nothing, but a master story nonetheless. Christianity, with its pattern of creation, fall, redemption and glorification, is a master narrative. I see my life and the lives of others as tiny chapters in that master story. The meaning of these little stories cannot be divorced from the master story, but some of this meaning is propositional. When, for example, I ask myself what I am really assuming about reality, the result is a set of ideas that I can express in propositional form.

The initial story in the present book illustrates one way a question requiring a nonstory answer moves through story into propositions without losing its story form. Notice what happens to the father when he is challenged by his son to explain why the world doesn't just wildly spin off in space or plunge downward to oblivion. He may not have thought about such an issue since he took earth science or astronomy in high school or college. He does, however, remember a bit about what he learned, and so he can make some progress. He can tell his son about the law of gravity. He can even tell him about the orderliness of the universe. What stymies him, however, is the ultimate question—what makes the universe orderly? Still, by pondering, he can make a stab at an answer. "Well, ah, er . . . uhm . . . it's matter and energy all the way down," or "God made it that way, and it's God all the way down." These are the choices a father in the modern Western world is likely to make. One is the first ontological presupposition of naturalism, the other of theism or perhaps deism.

There are, of course, other ways for the father to have answered his son's

---

[9]See chapter six in this book, pp. 113-14.

question. Let's say the father has made a full commitment to Zen. He is not yet a Zen master. He has not yet been enlightened or achieved satori. But he is anxious to steer his son in the right direction. So how does he answer the question, What holds the world in space?

"Son, that's considered an interesting question by those who do not know what questions to ask. Your teacher or something in you has started you thinking in the wrong direction."

"Why, Dad? What do you mean?"

"Why? What do I mean, Son? Even those questions are really unproductive. Come, sit with me. There, now get into the position you see me taking."

"Okay, Dad. Is this right?"

"Right? Wrong? Don't ask. It will do. Now, let us be silent."

The father may turn the boy's attention to an object in nature—the moon, the stars, a bird on a branch. He may teach the boy a mantra, like *Om mane padme hum*, or just have him say *Om* slowly over and over. But he will not answer his questions. Questions have no answers, at least not ones that appear rational to the waking logical consciousness. But after meditating, the boy may well no longer be interested in the questions. He may be captivated by the journey toward the Void—the empty fullness of the universe.

The first principle of Zen is that there is no first principle of Zen. Or, the first principle of Zen is Not. Everything in our conscious Western being cries out against the possibility that the father and son humming their mantra are remotely in touch with *the way things are*. Our presuppositions are so radically different that we have great difficulty seeing what the Zen father is trying to get his son to see. Perhaps we can't see it at all. Is there something there to be seen? If there is, then the Western notion that being is determinate—some specific thing and not something else—is wrong. No logic—no form of rationality—is common to the Zen father and the Western father, whether Christian or naturalist.

Here is where Dooyeweerd's notion of *ground motive* seems to me to be helpful. There is a commitment or disposition below the level of conscious reason that characterizes the heart of everyone. From this commitment flows the character of one's whole take on life. It generates the answer one gives to the first worldview question, What is prime reality? And that con-

trols the rest of one's worldview. James Orr saw this: "Everywhere the minds
of men are opening to the conception that, whatever else the universe is, it
is one—one set of laws holds the whole together—one order reigns through
all. Everywhere, accordingly, we see a straining after a universal point of
view—a grouping and grasping of things together in their unity."[ ] So did
Abraham Kuyper: There is a "need for all thought to proceed from a single
principle, a 'fixed point of departure.'"[ ]

Orr and Kuyper are, of course, talking about the worldviews of people
who are self-reflective and have some conscious knowledge of their own
worldview, though they need not know that it is a worldview. What about
the ordinary person who goes through life relatively unconscious of his or
her commitment to a view of reality? Is their worldview generated from a
single ontological conception? My tentative answer is yes, it is, far more
than they might think.

What, for example, is assumed by those who are not particularly
thoughtful about what orients their life? That thinking about such a topic
is irrelevant. It doesn't make a difference to what makes life work for them.
In other words, they have a subconscious notion that the universe (reality)
is basically benevolent. God, if there is a God (and there may well be), is
not concerned for their view of God. So even if God exists, he can mostly
be ignored, at least until one faces death. If God does not exist (and who
knows—he may not), then there is no need to worry about his nonexis-
tence. Again, the universe (reality) is basically uninterested in the worldviews of people. One need not worry about such issues. Nonetheless, it is
the ontology of such people, their notion of what the universe or God is really like, that governs the rest of their take on life.

That the "fixed point of departure" must be the one true God should go
without saying for Christians. As Dallas Willard says, "The single most important thing in our mind is our idea of God and the associated images."
Then he quotes A. W. Tozer: "That our idea of God corresponds as nearly

[ ] James Orr, *The Christian View of God and the World* (Grand Rapids, Mich.: Eerdmans,
1954), p. 8.
[ ] Abraham Kuyper, quoted in Peter S. Heslam, *Creating a Christian Worldview: Abraham
Kuyper's Lectures on Calvinism* (Grand Rapids, Mich.: Eerdmans, 1998), p. 92. Heslam
points out that Orr too "had an independent, unified, and coherent worldview derived from
a central belief or principle" (p. 93).

as possible to the true being of God is of immense importance to us."[12] Not just any God will do.

Assumptions which may be true. The presuppositions that express one's commitments may be true, partially true or entirely false. Since there is a *way things are*, the assumptions one makes about this may be more or less accurate. Perhaps, given our fallen nature, none of our presuppositions are held in such a way that they are completely and utterly true.

One could object, "But what about our belief in God? Surely that is completely and utterly true." So it would seem. If there is a God and we believe in God, our belief is a true belief. The question comes when we begin to put content into the concept of God. Do we have a completely perfect notion of what it means for God to be omniscient or transcendent? The very concepts stretch the limits of our mental capacity. As philosopher Roy Clouser says, "A concept of a thing includes everything that is true of it (which is why we never actually possess a complete concept of any individual thing)."[13] I suspect that we can be only partially true about most things that are possible for us to know.

There is an interesting biblical illustration of holding a correct presupposition and yet not holding the truth. In the Gospel of John 7—8, Jesus is arguing with the religious authorities. They believe that God is one. After all, does not the Torah say, "Hear, O Israel: The LORD is our God, the LORD is one" (Deut 6:4 NIV)? Yes, God is one. That's for sure. But Jesus has just made statements that more than suggest that he thinks he is God. That doesn't make sense. Jesus is a man. He can't be God. To say he is God is blasphemy. Jesus, however, tells them that they don't know what they are talking about, that it is they who are deceived. If they really knew God, they would recognize him as God's Son. So he charges them with not knowing God.

So what was wrong with their knowledge of God? Just this: They thought they knew *what* God could possibly be. They did not know that God's oneness—his absolute *onlyness*—could be a complex of at least two (later in John's Gospel, Jesus speaks of the Spirit, revealing God as a complex of

---

[12]Dallas Willard, *Renovation of the Heart* (Colorado Springs: NavPress, 2002), p. 100.
[13]Roy Clouser, "Is There a Christian View of Everything from Soup to Nuts?" *Pro Rege*, June 2003, p. 6.

three). The religious authorities' notion of God was partially right, but they extrapolated from this a supposed fact that was not true. They held it to be true, however, and thus they missed the stellar truth that God himself as Son to the Father was standing in front of them and speaking with them. Thus their supposed knowledge that God is one was false.

It is best to acknowledge that all our presuppositions are—as we hold and understand them—limited in their accuracy.

Presuppositions which we hold consciously or unconsciously. I have noted this so often that it doesn't need further elaboration. Suffice it to say that in our daily life as thinkers and actors, the bulk of our worldview is utterly unconscious. We are thinking with it, not about it.

Presuppositions which are consistent or inconsistent. This is undoubtedly true, but it is hard to document in any easy way, for once we recognize that our presuppositions clash, we are likely to abandon the offending presupposition, modify our idea, or modify the system so that the contradiction is either resolved or remasked from our consciousness. Still, I can think of one instance in my own mental development when I discovered a contradiction.

Early in graduate school I had adopted a radical form of New Criticism which said that the intention of the poet was irrelevant to the meaning of the poem. In my papers I wrote from this perspective. At the same time, I was studying the psalms of the Bible and assuming that the intention of these poems was precisely what I was trying to understand. I held these two views side by side and for months did not notice any conflict. Of course, it made no sense to read Scripture and not be interested in what its human writer, and more important divine inspirer, had in mind. Finally one day the contradiction dawned on me, and I changed my mind. Since I believed that my Christian faith, the content of which depends on knowing at least some of the intention of the authors of the Bible (and of God who inspired them), was far more firmly rooted than my recent developing literary theory, I jettisoned my acceptance of that aspect of New Criticism. This was fairly painless.

What is much more painful is to find contradictions in core beliefs. One believes that God is good but cannot reconcile this with evil in the world. Frank, a graduate student in literature, believes, on the one hand, that his understanding of the role of men and women in the church is largely correct and, on the other hand, that the social science he has been reading as a backdrop to his literary studies is basically sound. But he suddenly discovers that if the latter is a true reading of the way things are, the former is an ideological construct that oppresses women. This sets up a cognitive dissonance that demands resolution at a worldview level.

On a simpler level, Mary has fallen in love with Jeff and believes that she now understands true romance. She takes a course in psychology (which she takes to discover the truth about her inner self), and she learns that so-called romantic love is really due to the action of a couple of specific glands. Actually, it is possible for Mary to believe both of these so long as she keeps them in separate compartments in her mind.

One inconsistency is quite common. Some self-confessed Christians believe in reincarnation. I am convinced that those who do this have not understood very well just what Christianity teaches. For if it is true that each person is made in the image of God, then each person is unique. The doctrine of the resurrection of the body at the end of human history assures that each person is that same person and that person alone. But reincarnation involves the notion that one individual at death reverts to a state in which he or she can return as another individual in another body. This happens not just once but over and over. The two concepts of what happens at death—resurrection and multiple, perhaps eternal, reincarnations—cannot both be the way things are. One precludes the other.

If we are to have a Christian worldview, we will want to eliminate the contradictions in our worldview. We should, as Orr describes, strain after "a universal point of view—a grouping and grasping of things together in their unity."[4] That is what we should do. What do we actually do? . . . Ah, well, that's often something else.

The basic constitution of reality. A worldview, as I have said many times above, is concerned about *the way things are.* It is first and foremost an ontological commitment. It is the final answer to the question, What holds up the world? Every question—those that focus on epistemology or ethics or final meaning—assumes an ontology.

---

[4]Orr, *Christian View*, p. 8.

The close connection between ontology and epistemology is easy to see: one can *know* only what *is*. But there is an equally close connection between ontology and ethics. Ethics deals with the good. But the good must exist in order to be dealt with. So what is the good? Is it what one or more people say it is? Is it an inherent characteristic of external reality? Is it what God is? Is it what he says it is? Whatever it is, it is something.

I suggest that in worldview terms the concept of *good* is a universal pretheoretical given, that it is a part of everyone's innate, initial constitution as a human being. As social philosopher James Q. Wilson says, everyone has a moral sense: "Virtually everyone, beginning at a very young age, makes moral judgments that, though they may vary greatly in complexity, sophistication, and wisdom, distinguish between actions on the grounds that some are right and others wrong."[15]

Two questions then arise. First, what accounts for this universal sense of right and wrong? Second, why do people's notions of right and wrong vary so widely? Wilson attempts to account for the universality of the moral sense by showing how it could have arisen through the long and totally natural evolutionary process of the survival of the fittest. But even if this could account for the development of this sense, it cannot account for the reality behind the sense. The moral sense demands that there really be a difference between right and wrong, not just that one senses a difference.

For there to be a difference in reality, there must be a difference between what *is* and what *ought to be*. With naturalism—the notion that everything that exists is only matter in motion—there is only what *is*. Matter in motion is not a moral category. One cannot derive the moral *(ought)* from the nonmoral (the totally natural *is*).[16] The fact that the moral sense is universal is what Peter Berger would call a "signal of transcendence," a sign that there is something more to the world than matter in motion.[17]

Of course, naturalists, as much as Christians and other religionists, have a moral sense. If they were to analyze more fully why they have this sense, they might develop a cognitive dissidence that would lead them to change

[15]James Q. Wilson, *The Moral Sense* (New York: Free Press, 1993), p. 25.
[16]The naturalistic fallacy is well recognized in philosophy; C. S. Lewis has an especially lucid explanation in *The Abolition of Man* (New York: Collier, 1962), pp. 43-49.
[17]C. S. Lewis advances such an argument in *Mere Christianity* (New York: Macmillan, 1943).

their mind. But it is, as I have noted, always possible to have internal contradictions in the worldviews that we actually hold.

Provides the foundation on which we live. While worldview analysts note the relationship between worldview and human behavior, few, if any of them, make the lived-out aspect a matter of definition. That was certainly the case in my former *Universe Next Door* definition. In this refined definition I have tried to correct that deficiency.

The point is, our worldview is not precisely what we may state it to be. It is what is actualized in our behavior. We live our worldview or it isn't our worldview. What we actually hold, for example, about the nature of fundamental reality may not be what we say.

Here is a simple test. On one side of a sheet of paper, write what you believe about prayer. Now turn over the sheet and write down how much and how often you pray. Or vary that. On one side of a sheet of paper, write down what you believe about God that supports what you believe about prayer. Now turn over the sheet and write what your prayer life indicates about what you really believe about God. Christians are often less spiritual than their stated worldview would require.

An academic illustration is also apt. Often first-year philosophy students bridle at any notion that they have moral obligations. "What's true for you doesn't have to be true for me," they say. "Truth is anything I want it to be, especially with regard to ethics." "I'm okay. You're okay. And that's okay. Okay?" Nonetheless, if after they received good grades on their exams and papers the professor were to flunk them at the end of the semester, they would angrily protest, "That's not fair!" Relativists are always more ethical than their worldview would allow. There are no utter relativists.

WORLDVIEW: A REFINED DEFINITION, PART 2

The questions. The second part of a refined definition of *worldview* involves the list of questions that generate the specific worldview presuppositions. As I indicated in chapter five, I still believe the seven questions given in the first three editions of *The Worldview Next Door* are comprehensive. They cover the foundational issues in ontology, epistemology and ethics. I would still exclude aesthetics from the list for reasons of less relevance to how our lives are lived. I know this will disturb some of my very good friends (I know who you are!), and I will be happy to say, "Mea culpa," but still go on sinning. In any case, the seven questions remain.

Nonetheless, they can be expanded, fleshed out, as it were, to include the perspectives of the broad range of secular and Christian analysts. Here is my attempt to do so.

1. **What is prime reality—the really real?**
   This is, as I have not been afraid to repeat, the question of questions. The chief answers are God and matter (that is, matter and energy in a complex but determinate relationship). If God is the answer, then further questions need to be answered: What is the basic character of God—personal or impersonal (if personal, one or many), omnipotent or limited, ignorant or knowing (if knowing, omniscient or limited), good or indifferent?

2. **What is the nature of external reality, that is, the world around us?**
   From Robert Redfield: What is confronted? What is the nature of the not-man? What is the source of the orderliness of things? From Walsh and Middleton: Where am I?

3. **What is a human being?**
   This issue has spawned a variety of questions that a worldview is poised to answer. From Wilhelm Dilthey: Where did I come from? Why do I exist? From Walsh and Middleton: Who am I?

4. **What happens to a person at death?**
   Dilthey: What will become of me? (Dilthey says, "This is the most general question of all questions and the one that most concerns me."[8] I agree with the second half of the sentence but not the first.)

5. **Why is it possible to know anything at all?**
   I did not find this class of question listed by any worldview analyst, but surely it is a vital one. The answer links epistemology to ontology.

6. **How do we know what is right and wrong?**
   From Orr: Is the constitution of things good or evil? By what ultimate principles ought human beings to be guided in the framing and ordering of their life? What rational justification does the nature of things afford

---

[8]Wilhelm Dilthey, quoted in Naugle, *Worldview*, p. 83.

for the higher sentiments of duty and religion? What's wrong (with others, me, the universe)? From Redfield: What is humankind called upon to do?

7. **What is the meaning of human history?**
From Orr: What is the true end of existence? From Walsh and Middleton: What's the remedy for what's wrong? In what master story is the story of my life and that of all others living and dead? What story ties together all the elements of one's worldview?

THE DIFFERENCE THE DIFFERENCE MAKES

What difference does the refined definition make to worldview analysis? The main difference is a shift of focus from propositions and stories to the heart that grasps and understands them. With the locus of a worldview in the heart, we will be careful to respect the depth of its roots in each person. We will be loath to think simple arguments—or perhaps the most sophisticated of arguments—will dislodge any presupposition from its operating position in the life of an individual. We will be more willing to talk about *conversion* than of a mere change of mind when we see a person's worldview change. Some errors in worldview will become apparent and be eliminated only with much prayer and supplication. That will be true of our own errors as much as those of others whose views we try to change.

Second, the explicit presuppositions of anyone's worldview may not change, but their lived-out character will be emphasized. Whether we are looking at our own worldview, that of another person, or that of a whole society, age or culture, our attention will be drawn to the behavioral dimension. A society, a religion or a community may proclaim itself to be peaceful or equally honoring of men and women or slaves and free. A church may say it honors God and seeks first his kingdom. A nation may say it treats all its citizens equally. An individual may claim to believe in a God of shalom—peace with justice. But we will take into account how each behaves.

Third, because the mainstay of one's worldview is ontological, a commitment to a specific notion of fundamental reality, we will take a person's notion of God or nature or themselves to be the most important aspect of their character. Their support or rejection of any ethical principle—say, prochoice or prolife—is less fundamental than the notion of what is ultimately real. Christians proclaiming either ethical principle do so primarily from an understanding of who God is; each side will have a somewhat different notion—perhaps small, perhaps very large indeed. A change of position on this issue will mean a worldview change at a deep level.

In the final chapter, we will turn our attention to the ways in which worldview analysis can enhance our own worldview and provide a greater insight into how we can live in a pluralistic world—where it is not only ignorant armies that clash by night but intelligent people who clash by day.

8

Intelligent People
Who Clash by Day
WORLDVIEWS AS A TOOL
FOR ANALYSIS

. . . The world, which seems

To lie before us like a land of dreams,

So various, so beautiful, so new,

Hath really neither joy, nor love, nor light,

And we are here as on a darkling plain

Swept with confused alarms of struggle and flight,

Where ignorant armies clash by night.

MATHEW ARNOLD, "DOVER BEACH"

We live in a pluralistic world. Around the world there are nations where most people deny what our nation holds dear. There are religions in India or Asia or Africa that dramatically oppose our own, whatever it is. And there are enclaves of devoted ideological revolutionaries and terrorists who train for violent assaults on people like us. This *us*, of course, includes not only the *us* who are Christians but the *us* who are Hindus or Muslims or Marxists or secular humanists. There is no simple division between Christians and all others. The others are multiple. They too inhabit a pluralistic world. And in a pluralistic world it is not only ignorant armies who clash by night but intelligent people who clash by day.

Worldview analysis will not solve the problems of pluralism, problems that threaten not just to divide us but to destroy us; it will not bring us together. But it will help us understand why we are both so similar and so different. Without this knowledge we are like a diver caught in the tentacles of an octopus. We chop off one tentacle that has us in its clutches, only to find ourselves in the grip of another. We never really understand the heart of our problem. Worldview analysis brings the large picture into focus. It illuminates the heart of the matter. And it can help us to ferret out why we have such problems living with each other.

So we turn now to seeing how worldview can be a tool of analysis in four ways: self-analysis, analysis of other individuals, cultural analysis and academic analysis.

NAMING YOUR OWN ELEPHANT

One of the most important uses of worldview analysis is self-analysis. To become conscious of your grasp of the fundamental nature of reality, to be able to tell yourself just what you believe about God, the universe, yourself and the world around you—what else could be more important? You would be able to live the proverbial examined life. Naming your own elephant does not guarantee that you are right, but it does mean that you know where you stand.

When I have taught formal courses in worldviews, I have often asked students to do such self-analysis. This is an easy assignment, I think, and many of them do too. But some find it puzzling and even traumatic. For doing this well means asking not just what you think you believe about the really real, but what your life tells you about what your worldview really is. Moreover, self-analysis often involves identifying your major intellectual and emotional changes and developments.

In my own case, in broad worldview terms, there has been a wealth of development but only little change of direction. I grew up in a Christian family. My parents and my father's parents lived together in—I kid you not—a little house on the prairie in Nebraska. Religious instruction was limited to my mother's Bible lessons on Sundays and an occasional church service in the summer in a country schoolhouse six miles away. My world was that of a dozen or so surrounding ranches, a one-room school with a young high-school graduate as a teacher, a radio bringing in *The Lone*

Ranger and news of World War II, weekly magazines, and a handful of books, some of them very good.

Ranch life, rural life in general, is lived close to the soil. If it rains the right amount, the crops grow, the cattle have feed, the ranch survives. If it rains too little, the cattle slowly starve and the ranch is in great jeopardy. If it rains too much, the end result is the same. It is a hard life, not just in the sense of being difficult but in its being substantially real. It's real dirt you live on, real wood you cut with an ax and burn to cook and to keep warm in winter. I was always interested in books, ideas and the power of the imagination. But when I was growing up, I learned early that we lived in a very hard world. Is this the biographical reason for my instance on ontology's preceding everything else? Perhaps, but that does not make the notion less true. It justifies it.

My few religious experiences were all interpreted in the light of basically Christian ideas. For instance, once out on the prairie above our house in the valley, I saw three thunderheads rise from the western horizon and I thought I was being pursued by the Father, the Son and the Holy Ghost. By age ten or eleven, I had understood God as a Trinity, though I have no idea how I came by that idea. Certainly there was no depth to my knowledge of what that meant. I never remember, for example, being taught a traditional creed. In any case, Mom and Dad moved with my two sisters and me to a small town during the summer before I entered the seventh grade. We began regularly attending an evangelical church, and before the summer was over, I had walked the aisle at the pastor's invitation and given over my life to Christ.

My belief in God immediately became more personal, and I began to read the Bible, pray, and pay close attention in Sunday school, church and Youth for Christ meetings. It was not long before I had in essence the same worldview I described as Christian thirty years later in the first edition of *The Universe Next Door* (1976). It remains mine to this day. What has changed has been countless details, some trivial, some quite important, but all within the confines of traditional Christian thought.

Certainly, though, the growth and development of my worldview were aided not only by the increased quantity, quality and intensity of my exposure to the Bible and Christian theology but by the context in which that instruction came—a university world that has displayed vastly different and sometimes hostile worldviews. I remember, for example, being told my anthropology professor, "Sire, you read lots of books, but they are all the wrong kind." He was not entirely wrong about that, as I came to learn later, but there was no way he was going to sway me from what I knew personally to be true: the Bible is a reliable book, and God was in Christ reconciling the world to himself. My worldview remained solidly Christian throughout my entire educational experience.

For some—perhaps most these days—worldview analysis will reveal radical shifts. A number of Christians have written about their conversion in ways that show that more was involved than something only vaguely spiritual. I will name only three. Charles Colson, the Watergate conspirator, tells the story, in *Born Again*, of his shift in worldview from self-centered power-hungry materialism to Christian faith. He was greatly influenced by English literary scholar C. S. Lewis, who in *Surprised by Joy* tells of his own movement from early exposure to Christianity to atheism to deep commitment to Christ. Tatiana Goricheva, born into a pervasively Marxist world, tells of her disillusionment with communist ideology, her descent into nihilism, and her grasping for a way out in existentialism and then philosophical yoga. Her *Talking About God Is Dangerous* includes a dramatic account of chanting the Lord's Prayer and suddenly realizing that what she was chanting was not just a meaningless mantra but the very truth itself.[1]

I have been privileged as a teacher to have a number of students who were once Marxists or Maoists or more generically atheists, and friends who have been Hindus, Buddhists and New Agers. Their worldview stories are very different from my own. One of them is, I believe, worth including here.[2]

---

[1] See Charles Colson, *Born Again* (Old Tappan, N.J.: Spire, 1977); C. S. Lewis, *Surprised by Joy* (London: Geoffrey Bles, 1955); and Tatiana Goricheva, *Talking About God Is Dangerous*, trans. John Bowden (New York: Crossroad, 1986). I have summarized the stories of Colson and Goricheva in *Why Should Anyone Believe Anything at All?* (Downers Grove, Ill.: InterVarsity Press, 1994), pp. 192-95, 198-202.
[2] English is not the first language of Sixia Lu. With her permission I have edited her essay for publication here. I have retained her transliteration of the names of the Chinese people to whom she refers.

THERE IS ANOTHER SKY
Sixia Lu

> All the good things would not fade away,
> For all the beauty and the truth lasts forever;
> Although they could be frozen as ice in the heart
> Still comes the time that they are blooming like the flowers in the spring,
> One day, when HE passes by —

It is said that in the beginning we worshiped heaven. It is written that our Chinese ancestors used lamb as sacrifice and prayer as the way to communicate with the One who created the heaven and the earth. Then the lights from heaven shone across the clouds, and the sky looked like seven big stones with seven bright colors. The thunder came with fresh rains of blessing, and the season of harvest followed.

This land was then called China, and it is still called that today. China— the land of God.

Believe it or not, Nietzsche wasn't mad. In the land of God, God is dead. A third of the world's population has murdered him in their minds.

Believe it or not, if China today would open her mind, she would find another sky.

The Land of God Without God

"Therefore, the bird which is called Jin-Wei used her beak every day to put the stones and branches into the ocean. Finally, she made the ocean to become the earth." Mother finished the story, and then she added, "Of course, we all know that this is just a fairy tale. The world is just matter. Only what you can see, touch and feel is real. Fables, tales, myths—they are all the treasures of human wisdom. I told you the story to encourage you to create real miracles by hard work, faith and perseverance. Knowledge is power. Whoever has knowledge has the world."

That's the first worldview lesson that I had from my mother. I was six years old at the time. All my subsequent education strengthened and confirmed this as absolute truth: The primary reality is Matter; the world is autonomous; it has formed itself through evolution. When we die, we disappear into the air. Our duty is to make the universe even more beautiful for the next generation.

What, then, was real to me? Science, the things that happened yesterday, history, matter—these were everything that was real to me.

Since human beings can create miracles by their hands and hard work, why God? We don't need a God. If there is a God, he must be ourselves. Human beings can develop their knowledge. All things are possible with human effort. Besides, there are already a lot of gods in China. We don't need to import Jesus. Jesus was simply one of the "good guys" in history.

It's history that is real. It happened. And the wheel of history will never stop for anyone. It forever moves forward; there's no stopping it. We live and die without mercy.

Good character is necessary in our society—being polite, kind and warm to each other, helping the young and the old. "We must keep our traditional good character, but get rid of the boundaries in the corrupted old culture." That was the message of my education: the moral standards of socialism combine the best of the old and the new. This is what we should follow. Our country's leader was our hero, the best model for us. I didn't realize that the leader and the socialist moral standards had become our gods.

At the end of the 1970s and the beginning of the 1980s, the socialist ideal was for everyone to have the same rights; everyone was to be treated as a brother or sister. According to communism, everyone lives in one big family, and eventually we would realize our ideal: social equality, no war, no fighting, abundant food, enough supplies, total harmony, endless and total happiness.

This picture inspired everyone to be good. All private possessions and excess wealth were shameful and selfish. Speaking practically, this special cultural atmosphere created in me, and others too, a kind of happiness. I miss it now. I remember when no one locked their houses; yet no thief was able to get away. It was only later, when I grew older, that I realized that according to the "average wealth" policy, everyone in the nation was so poor that there was nothing for anyone to steal.

Like a string of pearls held together by a thread, every aspect of my basic worldview was shaped by this vision.

In appearance, in personality, I am still the same now as then, but my basic worldview has changed. And as that change took place, little by little every piece of my life changed. I still love to be kind and nice to people; I still laugh, cry, work hard and am confused, but there is now a strong sense of knowing where truth, beauty and love come from. I no longer have a limited internal desire to be good. I know that there is a source that provides a path for my life. My purpose for living has changed. I no longer desire to acquire more things. I am looking for something higher—to be like him—the infinite, good God. I am not trading my faith for his promise of eternal life. I simply need him to be the absolute truth in my life now.

The world without God is cold. With him, we know why there is warmth in the winter.

The Happiness of the Fish

About 380 B.C., Zuang-Cuo and Meng-Ji, two famous Chinese philosophers, were traveling together. When they stopped by a river, Zuang-Cuo watched the fish in the river and said, "How happy are these fish!"

Meng-Ji didn't quite agree. He said, "You are not the fish. How do you know the happiness of the fish?"

Zuang-Cuo replied in a famous statement that still affects how Chinese people think about human beings and their relation to nature: "You are not me. How do you know that I don't know the happiness of the fish?"

Meng-Ji is a disciple of Confucius, and Zuang-Cuo is a student of Lao-Zhi, the founder of Taoism. It is said that Confucianism and Taoism are the two-sided mirror of the soul for Chinese. In Confucian thought, people learn to be governor, manager and intellectual. It's the worldview which teaches that "the king is the son of God, and people must obey and support his reign." Furthermore, high virtue, obedience to all kinds of laws and respect for life are required. In this worldview God begins to be pulled from his heavenly chair and replaced by a national leader or a hero. With my whole heart I came to accept this Confucian/Taoist view of reality.

But Zuang-Cuo's Taoism focuses on the "self" and the oneness of the "self" with nature. He could not understand the huge power behind chaos and nature, though he sensed that something was there. Following his teacher Lao-Zhi, he calls the one who creates everything the Tao. Hence the term Taoism. For myself, I wonder just what kind of facial expression the wise man would have if he were to learn that God is the Tao, something he could not name.

Communism or Marxism is not the only worldview in China. Though it is the one taught in schools and the one ruling ideology, Confucianism and Taoism still cast their shadow on the land. Before I met the Lord, for example, I was no simple communist. I loved Zuang-Cuo.

Even before I was able to identify Zuang-Cuo's worldview, I was interested in his words. He is the artist of thinking, both romantic and wise. His attitude to life is soft and tender. I often felt strong pressure to be smart, intelligent, excellent in mind. But I did not always succeed. So when I failed, when I felt the coldness of people's hearts, when I became sick of the world of calm and self-control, I ran to Zuang-Cuo's world of being with nature—to hear the wind and the sound of water. With him I thought death is not so terrible; we just totally disappear from this earth. In his worldview, my spirit would return to the Tao, the oneness which unites all the other spirits into one.

There was a time, then, that my worldview was swinging between Chinese existentialism and Taoism. *I will work hard in school*, I thought. *But after school, I will ride my bike to the riverside, meditate on Zuang-Cuo's words and rest*. Absolute existentialism made me like a machine, but I am a human being and not a human doing. I need spiritual space. That to me was the happiness of the fish.

The Missing Land and Another Sky

Always use critical thinking to look at things. There is no absolute answer; the world is based on relative answers. Different people see the same object differently. The truth to you may not be the truth to others. Just be yourself. Do whatever you want to do.

In China the dream of "we are rich together or we are poor together" faded. With the open-door policy, we suddenly went into a period of economic expansion. Communism was still taught in class, but Marxism needed to be applied to life, and it wasn't. Fewer and fewer people believed in it. None of my college friends did, and neither did our teachers. The more we studied, the more questions arose. The theory—the ideal picture of communism—was perfect, it had been said. Then why wasn't our country moving toward that goal? Why was there more and more trouble in our society?

One day in my study group, all of us came to the same conclusion: communism is just a dream. We realized that if communism were ever to work it would require perfect human beings. We looked in shock at each other; no one could say a word. We knew that none of us could be perfect. What we had been taught was based either on a false dream or on a lie.

We had nowhere to go in our thoughts. What reality could we believe in? Even science could betray us, since people are not perfect. Even the most intelligent one makes mistakes. History is written by people. It too could be mistaken. We dared not go further. Believe it or not, the thirty students in my group broke out in sweat.

"Let's not think," one of the group leaders said. "Let's just try to do whatever we can to make a better life for ourselves. Let's improve ourselves as much as we can, make as much money as we can and enjoy life today. What's right and what's wrong is not important. Just be open to everything. Go for freedom." None of us were against this. A new page turned in our mind. From here on the intellectual postmodern world took root and began to grow.

"The ideal life is to improve the quality of life," some genius among my contemporaries suggested. Here came another wave to wipe away my thoughts: we need independence—economic independence, emotional independence!

Go!—Let's do business! During my last year in college, one teacher kept asking me, "Where are the two-thirds of this class that are missing?" The answer was simple: they had left to find a good job before they graduated, or they had gone back to the countryside where they came from.

Life is short. Let's have fun! And make good use of each other! Now came a whole bunch of party animals. And a frequent sight on campus: luxury cars picking up the young and beautiful women students. Why not? It's reasonable. Young women have the choice to choose a wealthy man. Women are free!

What is the standard for being good? With relative principles, nothing can be totally right or wrong. Everything has its own reason. Even a murderer has a reason for murder. After all, human beings are basically good, aren't they?

After the temporary harmony of a false dream, we entered a chaotic mix of competing worldviews. I was totally confused and lost. No proffered picture of the good life was what I wanted. Where is pure spirit? Where is clear thought? Are the saints only legends? Something was wrong, but I didn't know what.

Then one day someone read to me chapter 8 of Paul's Letter to the Romans. Here were the principles of the Christian life, the definition of love and truth. The first time I heard these words, I just knew that this was the truth about right and wrong that I was looking for. The tenderness and grace of forgiveness washed across my heart. It was all the reason I needed.

Romans tells us just how sinful our human nature is, how there is an infinite and good God. From my limitations I saw his unlimited power. History? Knowledge? Science? These are just pieces in God's puzzle. Life is more than just working, consuming energy and purchasing things. Life is more meaningful when one sees truth and love in the tongues and hearts of people.

Many good things returned to me—a desire to love freely, a passion to serve and a joy to search for truth. Knowing God brings me into a relationship with him, security and a restoration of my strength. Even difficulties have stretched me and made me grow. It's all more than words can express. Yet I will try to tell you what I see:

> There is another sky,
> Ever serene and fair,
> And there is another sunshine,
> Though it be darkness there;
> Never mind faded forests,
> Never mind silent fields.
> Here is a brighter garden,
> Where not a frost has been.
> In its unfading flowers
> I hear the bright bee hum.
> Into his garden, come!

This essay done as a class assignment illustrates a number of elements of good worldview analysis. Ms. Lu captures the personal and emotional tone of her understanding of her own worldview. She has seen it in light of several alternatives, and she has sensed the significance it has for her own life in a pluralistic world. Would we all could do as well as she!

ANALYSIS OF THE WORLDVIEWS OF OTHERS

Worldview analysis is also helpful for our understanding of the thought of other individuals. In fact, in listening to Lu, we have begun to do so with her. If we were to go further, we might read other things she has written, discover something about how she spends her time, and generally get to know her better. If we could talk with her, we could ask if she still thinks this essay represents her views. Where has she changed? What has become more settled for her? Where is she most puzzled?

If we wish to understand the movements afoot—past and present—in our culture, one of the best ways is to read the works of those whose thoughts, words and actions have influenced and are influencing our world. We can, of course, rely on the analysis of others, reading, as it were, essays on the essayists. Doing this is often helpful in discovering who is worth reading directly. Intellectual critics like Paul Johnson in *Intellectuals* or Bryan Magee in *Men of Ideas* and *Confessions of a Philosopher* or Jacques Barzun in *From Dawn to Decadence* can point one in the right direction.[3] Following up on the footnotes to *The Universe Next Door* can be helpful as well, as can the suggestions for reading in the appendix of my *How to Read Slowly*.[4] One will never run out of books worth reading.

A case in point: Václav Havel. Worldview analysis of people and their books can be quite straightforward. One simply reads with the seven worldview questions present, if not consciously, at least at ready recall. The most important question is always, What does the author say or imply about the really real? Begin to read, for example, the fascinating plays, essays, speeches and letters of former Czech president Václav Havel.[5] It will not be long before Havel's answers to key worldview questions come to the fore. Consider a brief paragraph from his address to the joint session of the Senate and House of Representatives in early 1990, just after taking office.

> The only genuine backbone of all our actions—if they are to be moral—is responsibility. Responsibility to something higher than my family, my country, my company, my success. Responsibility to the order of Being, where all our actions are indelibly recorded and where, and only where, they will be properly judged.[6]

---

[3]See Paul Johnson, *Intellectuals* (New York: Harper & Row, 1988); Bryan Magee, *Men of Ideas: Some Creators of Contemporary Philosophy* (Oxford: Oxford University Press, 1978) and *Confessions of a Philosopher: A Journey Through Western Philosophy* (London: Phoenix, 1998); and Jacques Barzun, *From Dawn to Decadence: Five Hundred Years of Western Cultural Life* (New York: HarperCollins, 2000).

[4]See my *The Universe Next Door*, 4th ed. (Downers Grove, Ill.: InterVarsity Press, 2004) and *How to Read Slowly* (Colorado Springs: Waterbrook, 1978).

[5]I have treated this topic in much greater detail in James W. Sire, *Václav Havel: The Intellectual Conscience of International Politics* (Downers Grove, Ill.: InterVarsity Press, 2001).

[6]Václav Havel, "A Joint Session of the U.S. Congress" (February 21, 1990), in *The Art of the Impossible*, trans. Paul Wilson and others (New York: Alfred A. Knopf, 1997), p. 19.

Two worldview issues are directly addressed, the first being most important. Havel's phrase "order of Being" is, of course, his name for the "really real." And for him, as for Christianity, Islam and traditional Judaism, the "really real" is the foundation for ethics.

What other characteristics does Havel attribute to "the order of Being"? A reading of Havel's published letters to his wife, written when he was in prison as a political dissident in Czechoslovakia, answers the question.

> Being . . . is not, therefore, simply a kind of nail on which everything hangs, but is itself the absoluteness of all "hanging"; it is the essence of the existence of everything that exists; it is what joins everything that exists together, its order and its memory, its source, its will and its aim, what holds it "together," as it were, and makes it participatory in its unity, its "uniqueness" and its meaningfulness.[7]

Havel here is alluding to some complex ideas one finds in Heidegger. He is more clear when he writes about his encounter with the order of Being on a tram late at night. He reflects on why he feels that he must put a crown in the slot even though it is late at night and no conductor is there to see him. A voice, he says, seems to address him, calling him to pay the fare:

> Who, then, is in fact conversing with me? Obviously someone I hold in higher regard than the transport commission, than my best friends (this would come out when the voice would take issue with their opinions), and higher in some regards than myself, that is, myself as subject of my existence-in-the-world and the carrier of my "existential" interests (one of which is the rather natural effort to save a crown). Someone who "knows everything" (and is therefore omniscient), is everywhere (and therefore omnipresent) and remembers everything; someone who, though infinitely understanding, is entirely incorruptible; who is for me, the highest and utterly unequivocal authority in all moral questions and who is thus Law itself; someone eternal, who through himself makes me eternal as well, so that I cannot imagine the arrival of a moment when everything will come to an end, thus terminating my dependence on him as well; someone to whom I relate entirely and for whom, ultimately, I would do everything. At the same time, this "someone"

---

[7]Václav Havel, *Letters to Olga: June 1979–September 1982,* trans. Paul Wilson (New York: Henry Holt, 1989), p. 359.

> addresses me directly and personally (not merely as an anonymous public
> passenger, as the transport commission does).[8]

These reflections are close, if not identical, to a fully theistic conception of God. Surely some Being that is omniscient, omnipresent and good, and who addresses you directly and personally, must himself (*itself* just doesn't fit these criteria) be personal.

Havel too sees this. And yet he draws back from the conclusion:

> But who is it? God? There are many subtle reasons why I'm reluctant to use
> that word; one factor here is a certain sense of shame (I don't know exactly
> for what, why and before whom), but the main thing, I suppose, is a fear that
> with this all too specific designation (or rather assertion) that "God is," I
> would be projecting an experience that is entirely personal and vague (never
> mind how profound and urgent it may be), too single-mindedly "outward,"
> onto that problem-fraught screen called "objective reality," and thus I would
> go too far beyond it.[9]

It is clear, then, that Havel's worldview is not so theistic as one might first have thought. Though he acknowledges the theistic-like way that Being itself appears to him, he doubts—perhaps rejects—the objectivity of these phenomena that he subjectively perceives. Havel has much more to say about his notion of "the really real," the nature of the external universe, human beings, epistemology, ethics and the meaning of history. But this is sufficient to illustrate the kind of evidence one can often find for identifying another person's worldview.

The exercise need not be just intellectual curiosity on our part. Knowing a person's general take on life helps us understand the reasons behind what people do and how they deal with specific practical issues. And that helps us relate to them in daily life.

A second case: Matsuo Bashō. Discovering Havel's worldview is relatively straightforward because he talks about his fundamental commitments. What about writers who do not readily do so? This task can be illustrated by the analysis of a literary work from outside our Western world. Let us look at a famous haiku by **Matsuo Bashō**, a late seventeenth-century poet.

---

[8]Ibid., pp. 345-46.
[9]Ibid., p. 346.

An ancient pond
A frog leaps in
The sound of water[1]

This is a deceptively simple poem, often learned and imitated by children in America as well as Japan. It is deceptive because from our Western worldview it appears to be a simple picture. It seems to carry no profound meaning at all. We may just as well be looking at a brief video clip. The scene is spare; the action is quickly over. What else is there?

Worldview analysis, however, encourages us not just to look at what first appears but to ask what mindset lies behind the picture. If it is a Western mindset, then indeed we have just what we first noticed: an image of a frog jumping into an old pond with an accompanying plop. But if we examine the worldview background of **Bashō** himself, we will find something very different. **Bashō** was a Zen Buddhist priest with a Zen mind. We will not be able to see what his haiku is doing until we examine his worldview.

The Zen mind is a Zen moment, a concentration of attention on a chronologically dimensionless present. It is the timeless intersection between past and future. It is and is not, neither one nor the other, yet both at once. Try thinking of the present in any other way. There is consciousness; yet this consciousness is always in motion. What one is conscious of at one instant is gone when one thinks about what it is.

Now all of this seems simply descriptive of consciousness. It is always conscious of something, but what it is conscious of is constantly changing. Consciousness itself is not a consciousness of itself; it is always of the other, and the other changes. What Zen does is to exalt this insight into a worldview. Zen proclaims that because consciousness is always conscious of change and never of permanence, change is all that is permanent; in other words, nothing is permanent. This is raised to a philosophic principle. The only permanent "thing" is not a "thing" at all. It is an absence of "thingishness." It is the Void.

---

[1] This haiku has probably been translated more than any other. I quote it from the translation in which, so far as I remember, I first encountered it: Donald Keene, *Japanese Literature: An Introduction for Western Readers* (Tokyo: Charles E. Tuttle, 1955), p. 39. For nearly 150 other delightful translations, imitations and takeoffs on this haiku, see Hiroaki Sato, *One Hundred Frogs* (New York: Inklings/Weatherhill, 1995).

Here we meet the crucial claim in Zen: human beings are capable of grasping all the reality there is. Nothing could be more opposite to the Christian worldview than that. Christians hold that there is much more to reality than can be directly perceived by our consciousness or dreamt of in Zen philosophy. God is there as the Creator of both our consciousness and the world of which it is conscious—and only partially conscious of at best.

What **Bashō** does in a multitude of his haiku poems is to create in us the realization of the nature of what he takes to be the "really real." How does he do this? Read it again:

> An ancient pond
> A frog leaps in
> The sound of water

Like many of **Bashō's** haikus, this one is pure image—image of sight and sound. The sight: an ancient pond and a frog leaping in. The sound: the sound of water. Not much. Indeed, but enough to encompass the whole of reality as Zen views it.[11]

The "ancient pond" is first of all a pond, not a symbol of anything. But it is ancient; it's been around for a long time; it carries the past in its present. The frog is first of all a frog, again not a symbol of anything; it is in the present. So both the frog and the pond together are in the present. The frog leaping is first of all a frog leaping, not a symbol of anything; the present moves. Then "the sound of water" is first of all the sound water makes when a frog leaps in—not a "plop" or a "bloop," though that is the way it is sometimes translated. In the Japanese the phrase is not onomatopoetic; it is just a phrase like "the sound of water." And that's important, for "the sound of water" makes no waterlike sound. The physical sound of the frog entering the water is not the sound of the words "the sound of water." The sound of the intersection of past and present is no sound, for sound takes time, vibrations are matter in motion. The interface between

---

[11]The following reading of the poem was suggested by Keene, *Japanese Literature*, p. 39, but I have modified and elaborated on it considerably. For comments by twelve critics, see Makoto Ueda, *Bashō and His Interpreters: Selected Hokku with Commentary* (Stanford: Stanford University Press, 1992), pp. 140-42.

past and present is not itself a part of matter in motion.[12]

By reading this poem, revisioning its setting and entering into its spirit, we can be teased out of thought. Our aesthetic experience then becomes a glimpse into what I take to be a major part of the experience of satori. So pause again: imbibe, read and reread this haiku. I am not suggesting this because I want to promote a totally Zen view of reality, but because there is an element of truth in it. Like a Zen Buddhist, we live in the present. Often we miss it. Let's allow ourselves a doorway into recognizing its subtle reality.

Here are several more haikus I have found as doorways into an appreciation of the present. I enjoy **Bashō's** haikus because they alert me not to the Void but to God's marvelous creation and the glories inherent in each moment. After all, there would be no conscious present if God had not created the world to be what it is and we to be what we are. If there are ancient ponds and frogs leaping, if there are crows on branches, if there are seasons, if there are gulls that cry out, then these haiku can help us see them in their presentness to us.[13]

> On the withered branch
> A crow has alighted —
> Nightfall in autumn.

> The sea darkens,
> The cries of the sea gulls
> Are faintly white.

> Such stillness —
> The cries of the cicadas
> Sink into the rocks.

Still, if we are to be responsible in the way we do our worldview analysis, we must also see these haiku as presentations of Zen. As such they give us a glimpse into the mindset of many other people, not just from Japan but from everywhere that Zen Buddhism has influenced people's minds and lives.

---

[12]There is one form of Buddhism that takes this notion so seriously that it conceives of the world as a string of pearls, each pearl created from nothing at each point along the string.
[13]These haiku, all by **Bashō**, are given in the translation used by Keene, *Japanese Literature*, p. 40.

CULTURAL ANALYSIS

When we turn to worldview analysis as cultural analysis, we turn from the narrow specificity of one person's worldview to the broad, much vaguer worldviews that characterize large numbers of people across considerable time and space. As noted above, worldviews have a public as well as a private character. The intent of *The Universe Next Door* has been to isolate the major worldviews that have a cultural embodiment primarily in Europe and the Americas. I have isolated seven such worldviews: Christian theism, deism, naturalism, nihilism, existentialism, Eastern pantheistic monism, the New Age and the most recent worldview shift, postmodernism. I have described these in broad strokes and do not need to do that again here.

But I do want to emphasize that these broad strokes both miss the finer points of our individual worldviews and somewhat misrepresent any one person's worldview. Even the way I have described the Christian worldview may constitute only my version of that worldview. In fact, there are times when I wonder if my description really fits me, for any one person's worldview is somewhat fluid. It is constantly under the pressure of being *worked*. We often do not live up to our so-called best lights. What we say we believe about prayer does not always represent what we show we believe by how, where and when we pray. Our worldview is also under the pressure of *workability*. Sometimes what we commit ourselves to just won't work. We then adjust our belief accordingly. Third, our worldview is under the pressure of new information, new facts and new ways of looking at the facts. In short, we change our mind, usually about small matters rather than big ones, but still enough that our worldview itself may be changed at least a little even at its roots. How we understand God as good, for example, is constantly under pressure from continued study of the Bible, from input from those more learned and wise than ourselves, and also from experience. And the presence of evil is always a challenge to our grasp of "the really real."

Nonetheless, it is extremely helpful to have a thumbnail sketch of the major worldviews present today, especially those that impinge on our lives through the conversations we have with others, the literature we read, and the movies and TV programs that we watch. Every editorial, even every news story, is written from a point of view, one that tries to be objective or that is openly ideological. Every movie and TV drama conveys a take on

life, some more obviously than others, but none with no worldview implications at all. Most sitcoms, for example, depict twisted and perverted lives
and values as if they were not only normal but right. The biblical God
rarely appears as a backdrop. Knowing what these alternative worldviews
may be helps us view movies and shows more wisely.

Every worldview described in *The Universe Next Door* is alive and well
and living somewhere in the world. It is in fact what makes our world pluralistic. When deism began to be culturally significant, Christian theism
did not disappear; when naturalism became dominant, both deism and
Christianity remained; when nihilism dawned in the late nineteenth century, naturalism, deism and Christianity were still present; and so forth. In
fact, naturalism remains today as the dominant worldview in Europe and
on university campuses in North America, while a vague, unsophisticated
deism dominates the broader North American world. Most people in America believe in God, but it makes little difference in their life; he exists as
someone or some force to get the world going and to give it order, but he
can be largely ignored in daily life.

Though the fourth edition of *The Universe Next Door* does not outline
the basic worldview of Islam in any of its specific forms, it has become important that people around the world become conscious of its major commitments. Islam's view of the "really real," for example, is of prime importance. God as solely One or God as Trinity; Jesus as human prophet or Jesus
as the divine-human prophet and savior; God as loving sinners or God as
loving only the righteous; God as forgiving us through the sacrifice of his
Son or God as being merciful without a redemptive action; human destiny
as inexorable fate or as involving some human choice; the Qur'an as God's
very words in Arabic or the Bible as God's Word through the instrument of
various languages. These are not trivial differences, and their implications
for individuals and culture in general are profound. We even need to understand various Islamic traditions whose views are different enough to
have caused violent controversy in the past and are the background for violent controversy today.

Worldviews in an Academic Setting
Early in my academic life, worldview analysis opened up for me English lit-

erature of the sixteenth and seventeenth centuries. I could read it, but I couldn't understand it until I grasped such notions as the Great Chain of Being (an intellectual model that forms the backdrop to hierarchy in both church and state), the Tudor myth that illuminates Shakespeare's history plays, the Copernican breaking of the circle and the ensuing rejection of the medieval model of the spherical universe (which makes sense of the poetry of John Donne). It was not long before worldview analysis became for me one of the most important tools of literary analysis.

Worldview analysis relates to literary study not just in helping readers grasp the meaning of specific texts but in revealing the assumptions of literary theory. Terry Eagleton's *Literary Theory: An Introduction* bristles with remarks, some of them reflecting deeply held assumptions, that are in conflict with a Christian worldview.[14] Here are only two of many:

> Literature, in the sense of assured and unalterable value, distinguished by certain shared inherent properties, does not exist.[15]

> "Value" is a transitive term: it means whatever is valued by certain people in specific situations, according to particular criteria and in the light of given purpose. It is thus quite possible that, given a deep enough transformation of our history, we may in the future produce a society which is unable to get anything at all out of Shakespeare. . . . In such a situation, Shakespeare would be no more valuable than much present-day graffiti.[16]

The not very hidden assumption here is that human beings have no essential common nature, that they are constructed by their language or their actions. Not so, a Christian must protest. We are what we are not by being creatures in society but by being in the image of God. There is a Presence

---

[14]With the influx of new literary theories predicated on sociology, psychology and linguistics, literary theory has absorbed a host of presuppositions that undermine every traditional literary theory, not just theories congenial to the Christian worldview. It must be the task of Christians to expose these presuppositions to critical analysis. Then when the various hermeneutics are turned back on themselves, they often can be shown to be self-referentially incoherent. For example, if, in accord with Michel Foucault, all uses of language are plays for power, so is the language used to say so. If power is not a criterion of truth (which it isn't), there is no reason to believe that all use of language is a play for power.

[15]Terry Eagleton, *Literary Theory: An Introduction* (Minneapolis: University of Minnesota Press, 1983), p. 11.

[16]Ibid.

that makes our identity distinctively what it is. Shakespeare—the writer who most fully displays the character of humanity—will always be able to be understood and appreciated, as will be Aeschylus and Homer, Cervantes and Goethe, Dante and Tolkien, Dickinson and Woolf. We grasp the humanity of those who left their marks on the caves of Lascaux thousands of years ago. There is a human nature.

In the past several decades, Christian literary scholarship has begun to become more self-consciously Christian, and while I have not noticed much use of worldview analysis in this scholarship, I am delighted to see it begin to proliferate.[17]

The field of philosophy is certainly the discipline where one finds the fullest penetration of Christian thought. Encouraged in the mid-twentieth century by Harry Jellema at Calvin College and Arthur F. Holmes at Wheaton College, Christian students have gone on to major universities, received their Ph.D.s and contributed at the highest level of academic performance. Working from the perspective of a self-consciously held Christian worldview, they have done important scholarly work in every field of philosophy.[18]

But that's literature and philosophy. How do worldviews relate to other disciplines?[19] The story is the same. Every academic discipline, including the sciences, is undergirded by a set of assumptions that may not even be conscious. Here are a few that relate not just to the sciences but to all disciplines.

First is the notion of the orderliness of the universe. If the universe is not lawlike in its operations, no theories can be tested even if they were able to be formulated.

Second is a reliance on the intellectual capacity of the scholar. The mind is assumed to be able to understand what it investigates.

Third, academic work since the Renaissance, rejecting the notion that

---

[17] See a survey of this work in Harold K. Bush Jr., "The Outrageous Idea of a Christian Literary Studies: Prospects for the Future and a Meditation on Hope," *Christianity and Literature*, Autumn 2001, pp. 79-103.

[18] I am thinking of such scholars as Alvin Plantinga, Nicholas Wolterstorff, George Mavrodes, C. Stephen Evans, Keith Yandell, William Lane Craig and J. P. Moreland (there are many others); some of their students now hold doctorates in philosophy and are making further contributions.

[19] The president of Union University in Jackson, Tennessee, has assembled essays from seventeen scholars on the faculty, each of which relates the Christian worldview to her or his own academic discipline. See David S. Dockery and Gregory Alan Thornbury, eds., *Shaping a Christian Worldview* (Nashville: Broadman & Holman, 2002).

we can deduce the nature of the universe from self-evident premises, assumes the contingency of the universe. The universe does not have to be the way it is. It could have been otherwise. So the task of understanding involves looking to see it more clearly, again with the assumption that the human mind is capable of doing this.

These assumptions cannot be proved, but they must be true if science is to give us genuine knowledge. This, in fact, has been accepted (consciously or unconsciously) by virtually all working scientists and, until the postmodern age, most other scholars as well. What is not usually noticed is that these foundational notions are not self-evident. For science to proceed, they are necessary assumptions, but they are not necessarily true.

When the young boy asks his father, "What holds up the world?" the father is forced to see that his answer is based on something he cannot finally prove or perhaps even understand. "God made the world to hang in space," or "That's just the way it is. Orderly matter and energy in a complex relationship: that's all there is." When one gets to the bottom, then, one is faced with naming the elephant. One must make a *pretheoretical* or *presuppositional* commitment.

The academic world is faced with the same questions and the same alternatives as the father. What holds up the world? Why is it orderly? Science itself was born from the Christian worldview that held that the universe is orderly because an omniscient and omnipotent God intended to make a world that reflected his own intelligence.[20] The universe is orderly because God is Logos (intelligence itself). That was a commitment—a presupposition—lodged in the heart of most early scientists. It is not the commitment lodged in the mind of most scholars now.

Today naturalism is dominant. There simply is no academic discipline—whether in the arts and humanities, the social sciences or the natural sciences—that takes as its starting assumption the notion of a God who has created both the scholars and the world they are studying.

"The Cosmos is all that is or ever was or ever will be" was openly stated

---

[20] Rodney Stark says, "Science was not the work of Western secularists or even deists; it was entirely the work of devout believers in an active, conscious, creator God" (*For the Glory of God: How Monotheism Led to Reformations, Science, Witch-hunts and the End of Slavery* [Princeton, N.J.: Princeton University Press, 2003], p. 376; see pp. 121-99).

by astrophysicist Carl Sagan, but it is the unstated assumption of every academic discipline.[21] God is not just unnecessary; he is irrelevant and even embarrassing. Biologist Richard Dawkins has only to say that fellow would-be scientist Michael Behe believes in God (which he does), and anything Behe proposes is automatically suspect, not even worth evaluating on its merits.[22] Naturalism reigns.

I think, in fact, that most Christians in the natural sciences, while being fully theistic in their overall worldview, are *methodological naturalists* in their scientific work. That is, they assume that as far as science is concerned, they do not need (and would even be encumbered by) the notion of God. Science deals with natural explanations of natural phenomena. There may be other explanations, but they belong in philosophy or theology or history or psychology or sociology. They do not belong in science qua science. God has designed and made the world; he has made us in his image. This explains the orderliness of the cosmos and the ability we have to understand it. But, they say, we do not need to call on any of this background for the scientific work we do. We can work alongside scientists who are metaphysical naturalists (that is, those who believe in no God at all) or pantheists (who believe that nature itself is divine), because the work we do does not require these metaphysical notions.

While methodological naturalism has been the dominant position taken by Christians in the sciences, it has recently been challenged by scientists and philosophers who argue for *design science*. This is not the place for me to take sides in this controversy.[23] My own view is that the issue is not yet —

---

[21]Carl Sagan, *Cosmos* (New York: Random House, 1980), p. 4.

[22]Among the scientists, physicists seem the most open to a nonnaturalistic understanding of the cosmos. Paul Davies, in fact, was awarded the Templeton Prize for Progress in Religion for his contribution to the dialogue between religion and science. Davies holds a panentheistic worldview; that is, he believes the universe itself displays an intentional mind. See his "Physics and the Mind of God: The Templeton Prize Address," *First Things*, August/September 1995, pp. 31-35.

[23]While methodological naturalism is still the reigning presupposition among most scientists, both secular and Christian, it has been seriously challenged by a number of scientists, philosophers and cultural critics. W. Christopher Stewart explains the conflict between Christians in "Religion and Science," in *Reason for the Hope Within*, ed. Michael J. Murray (Grand Rapids, Mich.: Eerdmans, 1999), pp. 318-44. For those opposed to methodological naturalism and arguing instead for "design" or "theistic" science, see especially the following:

and may never be—resolved. My only certainty is that God is always in relation to his creation as Creator. He upholds the universe by his word of power (Heb 1:3). John Henry Newman said it well:

> [Even though God as Creator is infinitely separate from his creation,] yet He has so implicated Himself with it and taken it into His very bosom by His presence in it, His providence over it, His impressions upon it, and His influences through it, that we cannot truly or fully contemplate it without contemplating Him.[24]

Christian scholarship undergirded by such specifically Christian assumptions may be an "outrageous idea," as George Marsden has put it, but that is because naturalism is such a powerful paradigm in academic circles. The suggestions Marsden makes in *The Outrageous Idea of Christian Scholarship* are eminently reasonable,[25] and it is a delight to see some of this scholarship on traditionally nonreligious topics emerge and contend in the marketplace of ideas.

At the moment naturalism reigns even in the field of religious studies. It is not God who is the object of investigation. It is *belief in* God. As one theologian at the University of Aarhus in Denmark once told me, "The systematic theologian at my university is an atheist." This is tantamount, of course, to being an astronomer who does not believe in stars but believes that peo-

---

Michael Behe, *Darwin's Black Box: The Biochemical Challenge to Evolution* (New York: Free Press, 1996); mathematician and philosopher William Dembski, *The Design Inference* (New York: Cambridge University Press, 1998), and *Intelligent Design: The Bridge Between Science and Theology* (Downers Grove, Ill.: InterVarsity Press, 1999); law professor and cultural critic Phillip E. Johnson, *Darwin on Trial* (Downers Grove, Ill.: InterVarsity Press, 1993), and *Reason in the Balance: The Case Against Naturalism in Science, Law and Education* (Downers Grove, Ill.: InterVarsity Press, 1995); and chemist and historian of science Charles B. Thaxton and writer Nancy Pearcey, *The Soul of Science: Christian Faith and Natural Philosophy* (Wheaton, Ill.: Crossway, 1994). Three collections of essays by a wide variety of scholars also focus on this topic: J. P. Moreland, ed., *The Creation Hypothesis: Scientific Evidence for an Intelligent Designer* (Downers Grove, Ill.: InterVarsity Press, 1994); Jon Buell and Virginia Hearn, eds., *Darwinism: Science or Philosophy?* (Richardson, Tex.: Foundation for Thought and Ethics, 1994); and William A. Dembski, ed., *Mere Creation: Science, Faith and Intelligent Design* (Downers Grove, Ill.: InterVarsity Press, 1998).
[24]John Henry Newman, *The Idea of a University*, ed. Frank M. Turner (New Haven, Conn.: Yale University Press, 1996), p. 37.
[25]George Marsden, *The Outrageous Idea of Christian Scholarship* (New York: Oxford University Press, 1997).

ple believe in stars, so that's what she studies. Theology then becomes the study of what theologians say or what and why people believe in God. In other words, theology becomes history, or anthropology, or sociology. People do not believe in God because God exists but because they are caught in a web of former belief, or they feel the need for a Father who is better than their own father, or they have not yet outgrown the need for a magical figure whom they hope will reward them, if not now, in a later life—or for some other totally natural cause. One must not say that these natural factors are not present, only that these are not all the factors there are, and that in fact the most important factor has been summarily dismissed. It is God in whom we live and move and have our being. Not to recognize that is to become futile in our imagination and have our senseless minds darkened.

ELEPHANT ALL THE WAY DOWN

The world today is marked by two seemingly equal and opposite characteristics. On the one hand, we are surrounded by people who view the world very differently from us. On the other hand, all of us hold so tightly to our worldview that it operates for each individual as if it were the only worldview.

In broad terms, for example, there are New Agers and atheists, deists and pantheists, Christians and Hindus, Muslims and Buddhists. The worldviews of each group lead them to live lives very different from each other. At the same time, within each group each person holds a worldview with unique features, often contrary to those of others in the group. Pluralism reigns both between and within groups.

One might think therefore, that no one would hold his or her worldview tightly. But that is not the case. Pluralism certainly puts pressure on everyone to adopt relativism, but mostly it does not succeed. In fact, each person in every group holds his or her worldview so firmly that, if we look closely, we can discern much of its character by what we see that person do and say. The fact is, however, that we usually do not look closely. As a result we often fail to understand why other people—even in our own group—vary so widely in their beliefs. *Why do they not agree with us more fully than they do?* we wonder. And in the United States almost all of us are still utterly baffled by the mindset of the terrorists of 9/11. Their actions are radically contrary to good sense as we understand it.

But what if we understand worldviews as I have defined them?

> A worldview is a commitment, a fundamental orientation of the heart, that can be expressed as a story or in a set of presuppositions (assumptions which may be true, partially true or entirely false) which we hold (consciously or subconsciously, consistently or inconsistently) about the basic constitution of reality, and that provides the foundation on which we live and move and have our being.

This notion of a worldview goes a long way toward making sense out of the seemingly senseless. It may not solve all the problems that pluralism presents. It may not teach us how to get along with our deepest differences, but it does make sense of our situation.[26] That at least is a beginning.

"It's Elephant all the way down," said the father. Yes, it is. And just what is the name of that Elephant? Whatever others say, we as Christians must respond: "The God of Abraham, Isaac and Jacob, and the Father of our Lord Jesus Christ is the Elephant." He alone is worthy and able to hold up not just our earth but the vast expanding universe of the billion and billions of galaxies the astronomers say surround our earth. God indeed is the name of the Elephant.

---

[26]See James Davison Hunter and Os Guinness, eds., *Articles of Faith, Articles of Peace: The Religious Liberty Clauses and the American Public Philosophy* (Washington, D.C.: Brookings Institution, 1990) and the papers in *The Journal of Law and Religion* 9, nos. 1 and 2 (1990). Both publications contain "The Williamsburg Charter," an important attempt to help us learn to live with our deepest differences.

Index

CPSIA information can be obtained at www.ICGtesting.com
Printed in the USA
LVOW11s0253030215

425440LV00001B/109/P